RUSSIAN PAINTING OF
THE AVANT GARDE

WITH THE SUPPORT OF

Foundation
for sport
and the arts

ScottishPower

RUSSIAN PAINTING of the AVANT GARDE

1906 1924

SCOTTISH NATIONAL GALLERY OF MODERN ART

EDINBURGH

Published by the Trustees
of the National Galleries of Scotland
for the exhibition *Russian Painting of the Avant Garde*
at the Scottish National Gallery of Modern Art
30 June – 5 September 1993.
The exhibition was initiated by, and originally shown at, the
Musée des Beaux-Arts de Nantes, 30 January – 2 May 1993.

© Trustees of the National Galleries of Scotland
ISBN 0 903598 35 3
Designed and typeset in Akzidenz-Grotesk
and Helvetica Condensed by Dalrymple
Printed by Balding + Mansell

Front cover: Malevich *The Scyther* (detail) cat. no. 53, pl. 16
Back cover: Lebedev *Geranium* cat. no. 46

7 PREFACE

11 RUSSIAN AVANT GARDE ART:
FROM NEOPRIMITIVISM TO CONSTRUCTIVISM
Christina Lodder

23 COLOUR PLATES

73 CATALOGUE

90 GLOSSARY

95 SUGGESTED READING

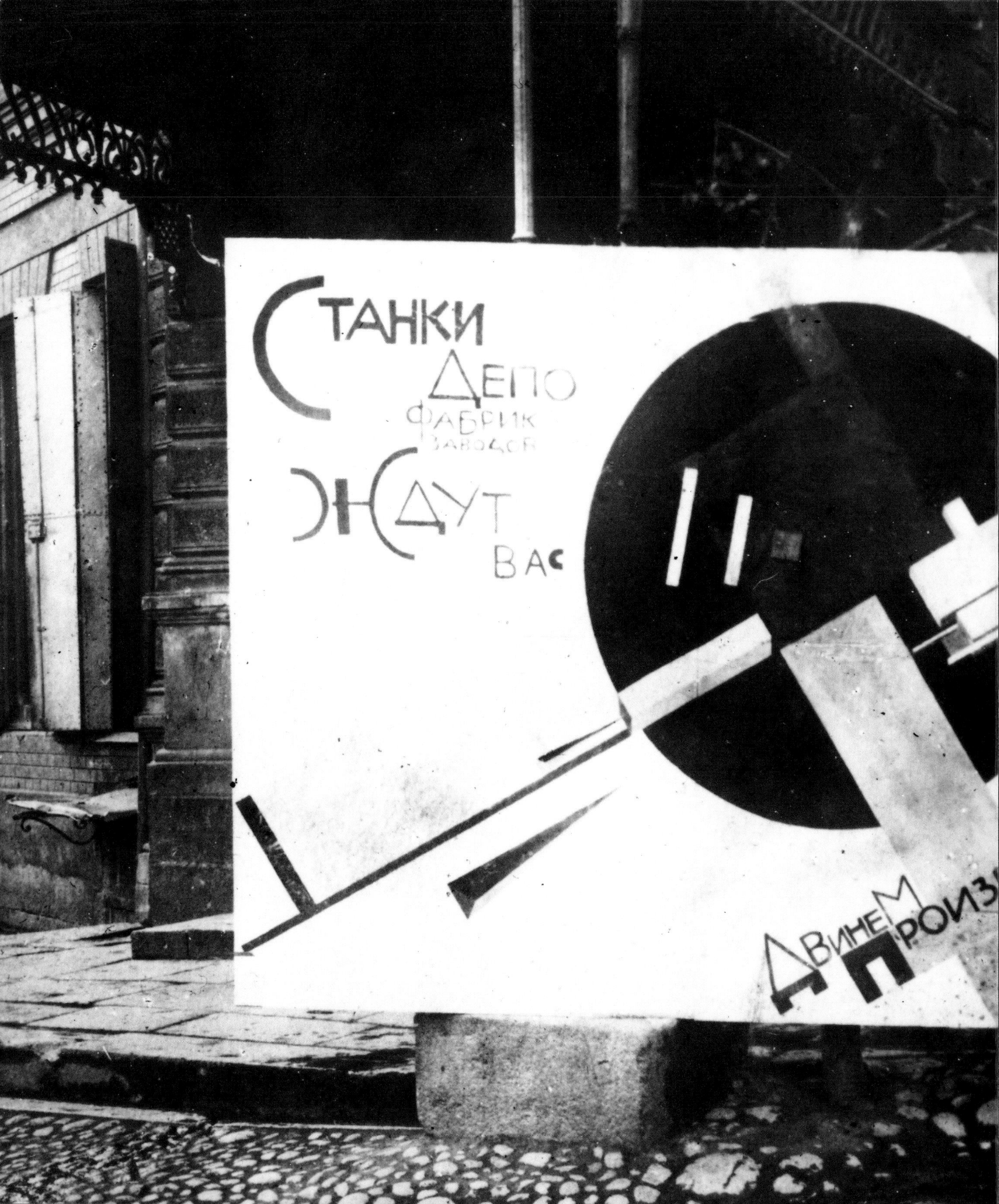

Станки
Депо
Фабрик
Заводов
Ждут
вас
Двинем
произ

RUSSIAN PAINTING OF THE AVANT GARDE
PREFACE

This exhibition would have been difficult, if not impossible, to mount before *glasnost* and the recent political upheavals in the former Soviet Union. We therefore owe an immense debt of gratitude to Vera Lebedeva of the Ministry of Culture of the Russian Federation, and to those provincial museums in her charge who have lent works from their collections. The exhibition was conceived by Henry-Claude Cousseau, director of the Musée des Beaux-Arts in Nantes, where it was shown to considerable critical and public acclaim earlier this year. Monsieur Cousseau was assisted at every state by Nathalie Brunet of the Réunion des musées nationaux, who also edited the catalogue which accompanied the exhibition in France: to both of them our sincere thanks. We are grateful too to Richard Mass and his experienced team at Pleins Feux Production in Paris for taking care of most of the administrative aspects of the exhibition. Once again, the Foundation for Sport and the Arts has generously supported one of our exhibitions; and we are especially grateful to Lord Weir, Chairman of the Patrons of the National Galleries of Scotland, for channelling funds from Scottish Power (founder Patrons) in our direction.

The story of how museums in Russia as far apart as St Petersburg and Astrakhan, or Tula and Nizhnii Tagil, came to possess such rich but, until recently, unknown collections of modernist art is related by the art historian Svetlana Dzhafarova in an essay published in the French catalogue of the exhibition. Between 1918 and 1920 nearly 2000 works of art by over 400 artists were acquired on behalf of the state by a special committee headed by Kandinsky, who, with Rodchenko, was instrumental in establishing museums of contemporary art in cities throughout Russia. Some 1200 works were subsequently dispersed to a total of thirty provincial museums. Henry-Claude Cousseau's selection of over eighty paintings from eleven of these museums reflects the extraordinary stylistic diversity of the radical art of what we have come to think of as the avant-garde years: the period between 1906, when the twenty-five year old Larionov accompanied Diaghilev to Paris, and the death of Lenin in 1924.

Something of the impact which advanced French painting of the early 20th century made on these young Russian artists will have been grasped by visitors to the magnificent Matisse retrospective in New York last year or Paris earlier this year. By 1913 the Moscow businessmen Sergei

opposite
'The Factory Workbenches Await You'.
Propaganda board in Vitebsk, 1919–20

Shchukin and Ivan Morosov had acquired, respectively, thirty-six and eleven paintings by Matisse, many of which were included in the recent exhibition. Parallel with their admiration for Matisse and the Fauves, the Russian artists found in certain kinds of ethnic art – icon and glass painting, shop signs, the popular broadsheet or *lubok* – an indigenous precedent for the flat primitivistic shapes and brilliant colours that they were beginning to introduce into their own paintings. Their rapid assimilation of Cézanne, Picasso and Cubism, and of the iconoclasm of the Italian Futurists, completed a reductive process which in the case of Malevich and his followers was to lead by 1915 to an art of total abstraction or 'non-objectivity' in keeping with the revolutionary spirit of the times.

That process is the subject of the present exhibition. There are in addition a small number of works which, in their emphasis on construction and using modern materials, anticipate the less spiritual direction which art took in the emerging Soviet society, when artists idealistically sought to integrate their discoveries with everyday life. Finally, the return to figurative art that gradually gathered momentum until it rigidified into official orthodoxy under Stalin is suggested by a handful of paintings from the 1920s.

To Henry-Claude Cousseau's admirable selection (about four-fifths of this exhibition) we have added a few works from British collections, including our own, that complement rather than supplement his choice – with one exception. In spite of his position outside the modernist mainstream and his exploration of specifically Jewish themes, Chagall seemed to us to be too significant to be left out of the history of Neo-primitivism. We were therefore delighted when Nicholas Serota agreed at relatively short notice to lend from the Tate Gallery *The Poet Reclining*. A masterpiece of Chagall's Russian period, it fills the gap perfectly and further strengthens what is one of the finest groups of Russian Neo-primitivist paintings ever to have been seen in Britain.

Ever since the *Art in Revolution* exhibition at the Hayward Gallery in 1971, and the news about the secret art collection in Moscow of George Costakis, so vividly revealed by Bruce Chatwin in an article for the *Sunday Times Magazine* two years later, museum exhibitions of Russian avant-garde art in this country have tended to focus on Constructivism and the post-revolutionary period. Commercial galleries, on the other hand, have consistently displayed major examples of Suprematist and abstract art – notably Annely Juda (a generous lender to this exhibition) with her memorable series of *Non-Objective World* shows in the 1970s. But it is to a book, published in London over thirty years ago, that we must turn for a proper recognition of the importance of Neoprimitivsm, and especially of the leading roles played by Larionov and Goncharova in the development of a Russian avant-garde: Camilla Gray's *The Great Experiment: Russian Art 1863-1922*. All subsequent historians of the cultural flowering that took place in Russia during those years, whether they realise it or not, are indebted to the late Camilla Gray's pioneering research.

It remains for us only to thank Christina Lodder, Reader in Art History at the University of St. Andrews, for undertaking to write this catalogue. As Dr Lodder says in her essay, the story of the Russian avant-garde is a complex one, with different stylistic groupings operating simultaneously and sometimes interdependently. Dr Lodder's text, however, is a clear and helpful guide through the maze of movements and individual names; and the order of colour illustrations, roughly chronological, has been chosen to reflect its argument.

TIMOTHY CLIFFORD
Director, National Galleries of Scotland

RICHARD CALVOCORESSI
Keeper, Scottish National Gallery of Modern Art

RUSSIAN AVANT GARDE ART:
FROM NEOPRIMITIVISM TO CONSTRUCTIVISM

Between 1906 and 1924, the Russian avant-garde emerged as one of the most vital currents in modern Western art, increasingly independent of developments elsewhere in Europe. In particular, Russian artists were at the forefront of the development of abstract art. Indeed, it is their complete liberation from recognisable subject-matter that provides a common thread linking the very different styles that were created under the labels of Rayism, Suprematism and Constructivism.

The emergence of these various approaches is a complex story and separate 'movements' sometimes overlap, both chronologically and in terms of the artists involved. Initially, however, in their reaction against naturalism and the Academy, Russian artists sought alternative inspiration in the advanced art being created in Western Europe, and also in certain native traditions that seemed to have been obliterated since the eighteenth century. The first product of this distinctively Russian artistic fusion was a movement which has been known since 1913 as Neoprimitivism.

NEOPRIMITIVISM

In 1906 Mikhail Larionov accompanied Sergei Diaghilev to Paris, where the latter was responsible for organising an exhibition of the last four hundred years of Russian art at the Salon d'Automne. At the same show, Larionov would have seen the large Gauguin retrospective, Post-Impressionist works and paintings by the Fauves. Subsequently, many other Russian artists visited Paris for varying lengths of time, meeting the major contemporary artists and studying their works. This stimulus was reinforced by the outstanding collections of French modernist painting that were being built up by the Moscow merchants Sergei Shchukin and Ivan Morozov and by the increasing number of contemporary French works that were being exhibited in Russia. The enormous Golden Fleece Salons of 1908 and 1909, for instance, contained works by Matisse, Derain, Picasso and Braque, as well as by Van Gogh, Gauguin and Cézanne.[1] At this stage, the Russians' experiments, shown alongside those of their Western colleagues, were still fairly tentative – installation photographs of the 1908 Salon reveal that Larionov's and Natalya Goncharova's works were still Symbolist or Impressionist in style. By late December 1909, however, when the Third Golden Fleece Salon opened, their paintings, which included Larionov's *A Woman Passing By* 1909 (cat. no. 38, pl. 1)[2] revealed more stridently modern characteristics, signalling the emergence of Neoprimitivism.

1 opposite
Malevich with members of the UNOVIS Group, Vitebsk, *c.*1920

2 above
Larionov and Goncharova at the Target Exhibition, Moscow, spring 1913

12

From the first, there was an aspiration to adapt Western ideas to create a national school, 'the rebirth of Russian painting' as David Burliuk expressed it in 1908.[3] Later, in his Neoprimitivist manifesto of 1913, Aleksandr Shevchenko acknowledged that 'Neoprimitivism was created from the fusion of Eastern and Western forms'.[4] Inspired perhaps by French interest in Le Douanier Rousseau and in African and Oceanic art, the Russian artists looked to their own archaic traditions: the eighteenth-century popular print, known as the *lubok*, as well as icon painting of the fourteenth and fifteenth centuries (figs. 3 and 4). In their disregard for one-point perspective, spatial coherence and anatomical proportion, these vernacular images suggested an alternative to the academic conventions which the Russian artists rejected. Shevchenko wrote: 'For the point of departure in our art we take the *lubok*, the primitive art form, the icon, since we find in them the most acute, the most direct perception of life – and a purely painterly one, at that'.[5] Although these were the prime sources of inspiration, other forms of folk art (embroideries, painted trays, toys, etc), as well as children's art and the work of signpainters like Niko Pirosmanashvili (fig. 5) were also very important.[6] We know that Larionov had a large collection of icons, *lubki*, Japanese woodcuts and other primitive works, and that he considered them to be of such aesthetic merit that he organised an exhibition of them in the spring of 1913 to be shown concurrently with contemporary Russian art on display at the Target Exhibition.[7] The range of sources, both Western and Eastern, that Russian Neoprimitivism drew on is evoked by the titles of some of the works that Goncharova contributed to the Donkey's Tail Exhibition of spring 1912: *White Peacock (Cubist style); Peacock (Chinese style); Spring Peacock (Russian embroidery style); Flock (Russian lubok style); Sketch for a Religious Composition (Byzantine style)*.[8]

It may be noted, in passing, that Goncharova was the first of a remarkable series of women artists whose acknowledged importance in the history of the Russian avant-garde is without parallel in other artistic centres of the period. The early evolution of her work epitomises the gradual synthesis of West and East. In works such as *Still Life with Green Bottle* 1909-10 (cat. no. 13), which relies on Cézanne for its perspective and brushwork, *A Provincial Landscape* (cat. no. 12, pl. 6), where Gauguin's more linear emphasis is explored, or *Sunflowers* (cat. no. 14, pl. 4), with its references to Van Gogh, the influence of Western painting, albeit freely interpreted, is clearly dominant. But in, for example, *Rabbi with Cat* 1912 (cat. no. 17, pl. 5), Goncharova succeeded in reconciling such interests with a bold simplicity derived from more indigenous sources. From icon painting, she incorporated such devices as the hand entering the space at top left, the expressive emphasis on the hands and face, the frontality of the figure and the way in which the white arch acts as a halo. The figures

3 top
Bold Youths – Fine Wrestlers
eighteenth-century woodcut *(lubok)*
Private Collection

4 centre
Andrei Rublev, *The Old Testament Trinity* c.1411
State Tretyakov Gallery, Moscow

5 below
Niko Pirosmanashvili, *Bego and Friends* 1907

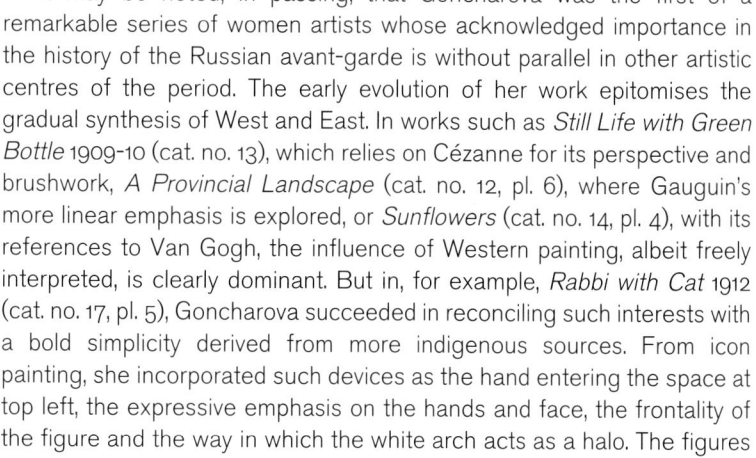

in the background, on the other hand, refer far more clearly to the *lubok*, as does the stylised depiction of the cat and the anti-naturalistic space of the composition as a whole. The work illustrates the fusion of such elements into an energetic, original and specifically Russian style.

The polemical force of such paintings was not always simply aesthetic. The Knave of Diamonds group was organised in December 1910 to spearhead 'the deliberate simplification and vulgarisation of forms'.[9] The name was taken from the flat, diamond-shaped designs on the uniforms worn by convicts, in order to emphasise the artist's position as social outcast.[10] This stance is reflected in the subject-matter of Neoprimitivist paintings, which was drawn from everyday life (eg Morgunov's *The Butcher's Shop* 1910-11, cat. no. 62, pl. 11), or from Russian low life and the underbelly of society. The latter is exemplified by Larionov's series of *Venus* paintings devoted to depicting ordinary prostitutes and represented here by *The Katsapskaya Venus (The Squaddy's Venus)* of 1912 (cat. no. 43, pl. 3). *Katsap*, a Ukrainian word meaning 'butcher', was a fairly pejorative term that the inhabitants of Ukraine and Belorussia applied to Russian soldiers.[11] The use of such an intentionally crude epithet in conjunction with 'Venus' immediately identifies the image with the squalid world of army camp life and commercial love, and carries overtones of national oppression. Appropriately, the cat brings out references to Manet's *Olympia* but also reveals the influence of children's art and the *lubok*. In Goncharova's *Rabbi with Cat* the figures carrying sacks in the background clearly refer to the pogroms against the Jews, which were incited by the Tsarist government of the time. The explicit use of icon motifs, especially the hand of God indicating that the Jews are God's chosen people, emphasises the holy qualities of the subject-matter and hence by implication the ungodly nature of the activity which forced these people to flee their homes. This makes the painting a very potent statement of political criticism. Indeed, the very choice of subject-matter was itself challenging in a state where Jews were denied many of the rights enjoyed by their fellow citizens.[12]

In February 1912, at a public debate, Goncharova stated:

Cubism is a positive phenomenon, but it is not altogether a new one. The Scythian stone images, the painted wooden dolls sold at fairs are those same cubist works … For a long time I have been working in the manner of cubism … [13]

Goncharova's *Peasants Picking Grapes* 1912 (cat. no. 18), with its crude vitality and radically simplified forms, recalls those 'Scythian stone images'. At the same time, its angularity, planar organisation and monumentality have affinities with early Cubist paintings such as Picasso's *Dryad* of 1908, which was by this time in Shchukin's collection.[14] In general, Neoprimitivism is intimately bound up with the first stage of assimilating Cubist experimentation. Malevich's *The Reaping Woman* 1912 (cat. no. 52, pl. 17),

6
At the Target Exhibition, spring 1913, from left: Larionov, Rabinovich, Obolenskii, Goncharova, Fabbri, Shevchenko. In the background (left): one of Larionov's *Venus* paintings

for example, combines simple cylindrical masses derived from Léger's version of Cubism with the simplifications and peasant subject-matter characteristic of Russian popular art. Modern French art and the 'primitive' married well precisely because they shared features in common; in this work the emphasis on the flat picture surface, the twisting of the limbs into a single plane and the fusion of viewpoints – the frontal view of the eye set in a profile face – could equally be attributed to early Cubism or to the native *lubok*. In Malevich's *The Scyther* 1912 (cat. no. 53, pl. 16) the figure is likewise rendered in a series of curved volumes, with an almost metallic sheen, but is set against a flat red ground that, with its decorative line drawing of fantastic vegetation, imitates the rediscovered woodcuts. Pavel Filonov's *The Three at Table* 1914-15 (cat. no. 11, pl. 12) applies a far more complex Cubist faceting to the depiction of crude and bulky figures with enlarged hands. The dematerialising effect seems here to take on spiritual connotations, and both the treatment and the imagery recall icons depicting the Godhead and the sacrament, such as the famous *The Old Testament Trinity* by Andrei Rublev (fig. 4). In yet a different way, Marc Chagall used the stylisations and anti-naturalistic space of both Cubism and the *lubok* to enhance the visionary quality of his images of feeling and childhood memory (eg *The Poet Reclining* 1915, cat. no. 3, pl. 14). In the West, Neoprimitivism is commonly identified with the art of Chagall but in truth his work belonged to a much wider pattern. Indeed, it is clear that, for a time, Neoprimitivism was the shared idiom of the emerging leaders of the Russian avant-garde.

Even a figure like Wassily Kandinsky, who was working primarily in Munich before the First World War, manifests affinities with this trend in his native Russia. In *Der Blaue Reiter* (The Blue Rider), the major collection of avant-garde texts which he co-edited with the German painter Franz Marc, Kandinsky included many 'primitive' images, illustrating *lubki* alongside African masks. The subject-matter of his early paintings was frequently based on Russian folk tales and exotic images of medieval Russia, as in *Cupolas (Destiny: The Red Wall)* 1909 (cat. no. 23, pl. 8). Moreover, from around 1910 Kandinsky often worked with imagery of the Apocalypse, derived from *lubki*, which he increasingly disguised or 'veiled' by generalising forms and accentuating marks, lines and patches of colour. The emotional charge of his original themes survives, however, in the visual dissonances and structural freedom of his compositions. Since the late nineteenth century, artists and critics had talked about art aspiring to the condition of music, with its autonomy of form and expressive directness. Kandinsky gave his paintings revealing titles such as *Improvisation 4* (cat. no. 24, pl. 9) and *Musical Overture: The Violet Wedge* (cat. no. 26). The rich visual drama of a painting like *Southern* 1917 (cat. no. 25, pl. 45) is vividly evoked by his own rhetorical assertions about the nature of art.

Painting is like a thundering collision of different worlds that are destined in and through conflict to create that new world called the work. Technically, every work of art comes into being in the same way as the cosmos – by means of catastrophes, which ultimately create out of the cacophany of the various instruments that symphony we call the music of the spheres. The creation of the work of art is the creation of the world.[15]

In his treatise *Concerning the Spiritual in Art*, published in 1912, Kandinsky argued that the artist should obey his intuition or 'inner necessity' in order to create works embodying spiritual values that would counteract the materialism of contemporary society.[16] He attempted, for example, to correlate different colours with particular psychological and emotional effects and also with specific forms and even musical sounds. Unusually, Kandinsky arrived at this vision of a completely abstract art without reference to Cubism.

RAYISM AND CUBO-FUTURISM

For artists and critics based in Russia, a more complex and up to date view of current Western art became available during 1912-13. Gleizes and Metzinger's explanatory text *Du Cubisme* appeared in two Russian translations during 1913; by the end of the same year Shchukin owned twelve Cubist works and Morozov had purchased Picasso's 1910 *Portrait of Vollard*. While some Russian artists like Robert Falk and Petr Konchalovskii interpreted the lessons of Cubism very much in a Cézannist spirit, others embraced this latest style more wholeheartedly. Alexandra Exter's *A Bank of the Seine* c.1912 (cat. no. 6, pl. 18), for instance, lies fairly solidly within the idiom of Cubist landscape. Similarly, Le Dantyu's portraits (cat. nos. 47, 48 [pl. 21] and 49) use the muted tones and geometrically defined facets of Cubism, although the latter appear to overlay the image, rather than serving to analyse space and volume.

Other works emanated from a more ambitious project to absorb Cubism and Futurism simultaneously. A report on Italian Futurism had been published in the journal *Apollo* in 1910 together with a translation of 'Futurist Painting: The Technical Manifesto'. In 1912 this manifesto was republished in the *Union of Youth* journal alongside the Futurists' introduction to their 1912 touring exhibition. In early 1914 Marinetti visited Moscow and St Petersburg, an occasion marked by the publication of two collections of Futurist manifestos. From being an artistic backwater, Russia was clearly now becoming one of the key centres of modern art.

For Larionov and Goncharova, seeking a path of development beyond Neoprimitivism, the creation of Rayism represented a distinct and original response to these new stimuli, despite Larionov's description of the style in 1913 as a synthesis of 'Cubism, Futurism and Orphism'.[17] The stated aim was the depiction of 'the spatial forms arising from the intersection of the reflected rays of various objects'.[18] Larionov asserted that the forms were 'chosen by the artist's will' and that the paintings were intended to be self-sufficient, 'free from concrete forms, existing and developing according to painterly laws'.[19] He seems to have developed this style during 1912.[20] Rayism was presented as a fully developed method at the Target Exhibition in spring 1913 and the catalogue contained definitions of the new style. These early Rayist works were later described as 'Realistic Rayism', in so far as they were still based on legible images. Such references disappear in 'Pneumo-Rayism' where the pictorial elements become more autonomous. Works like *Rayist Composition: Domination of Red* 1912-13 (fig. 7) are indeed completely abstract, composed entirely of coloured lines which are applied with a certain degree of gestural freedom. When Rayism was shown in Paris in 1914 Apollinaire said it 'brought a new refinement not only to Russian painting but to European painting as a whole'.[21]

There was a marked stylistic divergence between Rayism and Cubo-Futurism, a term possibly coined by Malevich. In spring 1913 Malevich declared: 'I consider Cubo-Futurism as the only possible way out and announce that those who will not step onto this path will be candidates for the cemetery'.[22] In general, Cubo-Futurism too represented a creative synthesis: from Cubism it took the new ideas of pictorial space, the fragmentation of the object, and the emphasis on geometric form; from Futurism an iconoclastic ethos, an emphasis on urban and industrial subject-matter and the dynamism of modern experience of time and space. Such concerns are evident in *Life in the Grand Hotel* 1913-14 (cat. no. 27), traditionally attributed to Malevich but more probably painted by Klyun.[23] Here the central figure is intersected by rays of light, conceivably suggesting a rotating door. Mikhail Menkov's *Tram No.6* (cat. no. 60) also captures the excitement of the contemporary city. Machine components, tram lines, numbers and rectilinear configurations, referring either to the buildings outside or the interior of the tram itself, all suggest the sensation of movement through brightly lit city streets. In Olga Rozanova's *The City* 1913 (cat. no. 80) individual elements retain their identity to some extent – a bridge, a train, a factory chimney – yet they intersect and fuse into a vortex-like structure, more powerfully evoking the dynamic energies at the heart of the modern world. The flux of individual experience is more the theme of Lyubov Popova's *Futurist Portrait* 1914-15 (cat. no. 66, pl. 25).[24] The head is fragmented to incorporate different viewpoints, while the contemporary environment is indicated through the use of collage (newspaper and wallpaper applied to the canvas), an idea borrowed from Cubism, as is the bold superimposed lettering 'CUB FUTURISMO', which acts like a declaration of artistic commitment.

7
Mikhail Larionov, *Rayist Composition: Domination of Red* 1912-13
Museum of Modern Art, New York

8
Olga Rozanova, Poster for the Union of Youth's *First Productions by the Theatrical Futurists in the World*, Luna Park Theatre, St. Petersburg, December 1913

SUPREMATISM

During 1913 Malevich, an increasingly influential figure, began to be more closely linked with Mikhail Matyushin and the Union of Youth group based in St. Petersburg. This resulted in his collaboration on the opera *Victory Over the Sun*, performed in December 1913, for which he created the Cubo-Futurist decor, Matyushin the music, Velimir Khlebnikov the prologue, and Aleksei Kruchenykh the libretto. Malevich's closer contact with the Russian literary Futurists had a clear impact on his thinking and on his development of 'alogical' painting, and eventually of abstraction. Crucial for this was the concept of *zaum*, which means trans-sense or trans-reason and denotes the irrational. Developed by the poets Khlebnikov and Kruchenykh, *zaum* entailed rejecting the conventional meanings of words and sentences, and asserting that the component elements of words, syllables and sounds formed a type of universally comprehensible proto-language which it was the task of the poet to reclaim. In November 1913 Malevich adopted the phrase 'transrational realism' (*zaumnyi realizm*) to describe Cubo-Futurist works such as *The Knifegrinder* c.1913 (Yale University Art Gallery) and *The Perfected Portrait of Ivan Klyun* 1913 (State Russian Museum, St. Petersburg), the latter of which has affinities with Klyun's own *Self Portrait with Saw* 1914 (cat. no. 28, pl. 24).[25] Clearly Malevich saw a corollary between the poets' destruction of linguistic structures and his own fragmentation of the object and emphasis on the automony of pictorial elements. After briefly producing Alogist paintings in which unrelated objects are juxtaposed at completely different scales (eg *An Englishman in Moscow* 1914, fig. 10), Malevich used abstract colour planes to overlay more descriptive passages (eg *Woman at a Poster Column* 1914, Stedelijk Museum, Amsterdam). Such an approach is paralleled in this exhibition by Rozanova's *Clock and Cards (The Gambler's Dream)* c.1915 (cat. no. 85, pl. 28).

In December 1915, at The Last Futurist Exhibition 0.10 (Zero-Ten), Malevich revealed a dramatic breakthrough when he exhibited thirty-nine totally abstract works comprising flatly painted planes of colour on white grounds, exemplified by *Suprematism* (cat. no. 54, pl. 32). At one extreme, he placed a large black square in the centre of a square canvas, implying an artistic *tabula rasa*; at the other, he devised complex compositions from shapes varied in colour, scale and geometric regularity. The latter paintings in particular are richly suggestive of space and movement.

At the same time as the exhibition, Malevich published a manifesto entitled *From Cubism and Futurism to Suprematism*.[26] With a rhetoric to match Kandinsky's, he announced: 'I transformed myself in the zero of form and emerged from nothing to creation, that is to Suprematism, to the new realism in painting – to non-objective creation'. He characterised Suprematism as 'the pure art of painting', in which pictorial elements have

9 top
Alogical portrait of the Futurists, St Petersburg, December 1913, from left: Filonov, Matyushin, Kruchenykh, Malevich, Shkolnik

10 centre
Kazimir Malevich, *An Englishman in Moscow* 1914 Stedelijk Museum, Amsterdam

11 below
Paintings by Malevich at the Last Futurist Exhibition 0.10 (Zero Ten), Petrograd, December 1915

their own reality, in contrast to the 'old realism' of imitation. This does not mean that Malevich was interested only in formal effects for their own sake. He asserted, for example, that the new artistic language encapsulated the essential spirit of the contemporary world of speed and machinery. The Italian Futurists inspired his affirmation of the modern world, but he felt that, in practice, their art had been limited by its descriptive approach: '... in pursuing the form of aeroplanes or automobiles, we shall always be anticipating new cast-off forms of technical life ...'. For Malevich, it was necessary to create a more abstract equivalent.

The artist can be a creator only when the forms in his pictures have nothing in common with nature. For art is the ability to construct, not on the interrelation of form and colour, and not on an aesthetic basis of beauty in composition, *but on the basis of weight, speed and the direction of movement.*

In the catalogue to 0.10, Malevich gave some paintings titles which mention the fourth dimension.[27] Certain French Cubists had talked about the fourth dimension, and Matyushin had linked their ideas with the hyperspace philosophy of Petr Uspenskii, liberally quoting from the latter's book *Tertium Organum* which stressed the spiritual as well as the scientific nature of the fourth dimension.[28] Malevich was closely allied with Matyushin from 1913 onwards and evidently discussed these ideas with him. Moreover, in 1915 Malevich made it clear to his Russian audience that he was asserting a transcendental truth by hanging his *Black Rectangle* (better known as *The Black Square*), which he called 'the icon of my time',[29] in the corner of the room, in the position traditionally occupied by an icon in Orthodox homes. Subsequently he developed images of a single form fading into the white ground, and in 1917-18 painted his series of white on white paintings which create an even stronger sensation of immateriality and infinite space.

From 1916 Suprematism had an immediate and profound impact on a whole range of artists who had previously been working in Cubo-Futurist idioms. Popova began to explore the possibilities of a purely abstract vocabulary. In some works she treated the forms like collage elements, layering them one on the other to produce densely structured compositions, as for instance in her *Pictorial Architectonics* 1916 (cat. no. 68, pl. 34). In her most original works she produced powerful, dynamic arrangements of boldly coloured intersecting geometrical planes (eg cat. nos. 69 [pl. 40] and 70). Rozanova too created striking and inventive paintings such as the monumental *Non-Objective Composition (Flight of an Aeroplane)* 1916 (cat. no. 86), built up of contrasting colours and shapes. The densely organised forms create the sensation of a vortex of movement, quite different from the floating quality of Malevich's Suprematist paintings. Malevich's emphasis on the autonomy of each pictorial element also led

12
Poster for the First Exhibition of Paintings
Tramway V, Petrograd, March 1915

Aleksandr Rodchenko to produce series of paintings which explore, with radical simplicity, the structural possibilites of line, form and colour. Rodchenko's rigorous investigations are represented in this exhibition by *Triangles* 1918 (cat. no. 75), *Non-Objective Composition* 1918 (cat. no. 77) and *Study for Non-Objective Composition No. 61* 1918 (cat. no. 76). Rodchenko even created a series of black on black canvases in response to Malevich's white on white paintings. As in the case of Popova, Rodchenko evolved a pronounced interest in painterly texture, and in the use of tonal modelling to create sensations of light.

When El Lissitzky encountered Malevich's ideas in 1919, he began to realise Suprematism's three-dimensional potential, evolving the concept of the PROUN (Project for the Affirmation of the New) which he defined as 'an interchange station between painting and architecture'.[30] In his works, which are highly impersonal in technique, diagonal configurations of precise abstract shapes evoke a visionary realm of futuristic cities and engineering structures, as epitomised by his Kestner Portfolio of lithographs of 1923 (cat. no. 51). Such diversity of experiments suggests that for a number of years, following Malevich's invention of Suprematism, Russia was one of the most important centres for the exploration of abstract art.

13
At the Rafalovich family dacha near Moscow, *c*.1915: Tatlin (centre, smoking pipe); standing behind him: Klyun (left) and Malevich

CONSTRUCTIVISM

Malevich remained the dominant influence on the Russian avant-garde until 1919-20. The emergence of a self-styled Constructivist movement in 1921, on the other hand, owed more to the inspiration of Vladimir Tatlin and his work with real materials in space. In May 1914 Tatlin had exhibited his first three-dimensional reliefs, which had been inspired by the Cubist collages and constructions that he had seen in Paris that spring. As his reliefs became totally abstract, the materials and their textures became the subject-matter of the works, which also established far more active relationships with their spatial environments. *Corner Counter Relief* of 1914-15 (fig. 14), for instance, is built up in space around two intersecting metal planes suspended across the corner of a room, enabling Tatlin also to highlight the iconic status of his artistic inventions. With such works Tatlin established 'construction' as an artistic method amongst the Russian avant-garde, as well as the notion of *faktura* or texture.

Other artists built upon these ideas. Władysław Strzemiński, for instance, in *The Meter* 1919 (cat. no. 97, pl. 43), used materials associated directly with contemporary technology. He employed industrially produced objects as integral elements of the composition, notably the ceramic insulators and flex needed for electrical circuitry. These were applied to a surface which is otherwise relatively flat, and they interact with the various pictorial textures which have been carefully produced by the artist.

14
Vladimir Tatlin, *Corner Counter Relief*
1914-15
State Russian Museum, St Petersburg

Similarly, Sofya Dymshits-Tolstaya's *Composition of a Compass* 1919 (cat. no. 5, pl. 42) analyses the action of a specific scientific instrument. Although the three-dimensional additions (the sand and stringing) are fairly limited in depth, the use of stringing going through the canvas is as technically innovative as her reliefs constructed from painted sheets of glass. The emphasis in both works on the aesthetic appropriation of machine technology seems to have been associated with the Revolution, and with the perception that industrial manufacture represented the origin of the working class, the new rulers of Russia, and the source of its power to endure and survive.

It is in this type of work that we begin to see the impact of the momentous political events taking place in Russia. The October Revolution of 1917, the overthrow of the Tsarist autocracy and the establishment of a socialist state, had a tremendous impact on artists. In the ensuing three years, while the Civil War was being fought, the avant-garde ran the Department of Fine Arts (IZO) within the Commissariat for Englightenment (Narkompros). Artists like Kandinsky and Rodchenko were responsible for purchasing works of art for the State and distributing them to provincial museums, including many of the works in the present exhibition. The avant-garde also used their art to fulfil the needs of the new regime, decorating the cities for the revolutionary festivals (1 May and 7 November), designing propaganda posters and creating sculptures to replace Tsarist monuments (eg cat. no. 101). Such activities led them to see themselves as the interpreters of the socialist message and the creators of the socialist environment, and to equate their artistic innovations with the political and social revolution.

The new aspirations were best expressed by Tatlin's *Model for a Monument to the Third International* (fig. 15). Commissioned in 1919 as a monument to the Revolution, this extraordinary structure was exhibited in November 1920 in Petrograd and then in Moscow the following month. Although the model was only about five metres high, Tatlin intended the final construction to be higher than the Eiffel Tower and to straddle the River Neva in Petrograd. The external iron framework, which spiralled upwards at the angle of the world's axis, created a powerful image of dynamism and progress. Within it were to be suspended three enormous glazed volumes, to house the various bodies of the Third International, an organisation devoted to promoting world revolution. Remarkably, these were to rotate at various speeds, the lower cylinder, where the legislature would meet, once a year, the middle pyramid, intended for meetings of the executive, once a month, and the upper cylinder, dedicated to propaganda functions, was to complete one revolution per day. The Tower would combine the geometric clarity of the new abstract art with industrial materials and technology, synthesising 'the principles of architecture,

15
Tatlin's *Model for a Monument to the Third International* on exhibition at the Academy of Arts, Petrograd, November 1920 (Tatlin is seen in the foreground holding a pipe)

sculpture and painting' and 'uniting purely artistic forms with utilitarian intentions'.[31]

Inspired by Tatlin's call for artists to 'take control over the forms encountered in everyday life',[32] the First Working Group of Constructivists was established in March 1921 by Aleksei Gan, Rodchenko, Varvara Stepanova and others – the first appearance anywhere of the term Constructivism. The group, which pledged its allegiance to 'marxist materialism', rejected art as a bourgeois commodity, replacing it with 'intellectual production', which would harness artistic skills to designing everyday items for industrial manufacture and so help in the creation of the new socialist environment.[33] In practice, because no advanced industrial base existed in Russia, the group went on to design furniture, theatre sets and exhibitions and to exploit photomontage and bold layouts in their advertising and propaganda work. By 1922 other artists had come to share the Constructivists' objectives. Popova and Stepanova, convinced that 'a cotton print is as much a product of artistic culture as a painting',[34] worked at the First Textile Print Factory in Moscow, applying their abstract pictorial language to devising textile designs for mass production. In accordance with the Constructivists' industrial imperative, traditional floral patterns were discarded in favour of the 'geometricisation of form'.[35] The designs were based on economical combinations of one or more colours and simple geometric forms. In a typical example (cat. no. 73), Popova interlaced yellow and pink circles with vertical black lines of varying thickness, reinforcing the sense of spatial dynamism through the introduction of a diagonal break in the pattern. During the 1920s, however, the Party leaders made it increasingly clear through their pronouncements and patronage of realistic groups that they had no patience with experimental approaches; rather they wanted a traditionally figurative art that would be comprehensible to the masses. One response to this demand for comprehensibility was an increased use of photomontage by the avant-garde. The photograph was a figurative image but at the same time it was machine made, it was infinitely reproducible, it had none of the *cachet* of the unique work of art and it could be integrated into highly abstract formal structures. Towards the end of the 1920s photomontage was yoked to the propaganda requirements of the First Five Year Plan through the poster designs and documentary albums of Rodchenko and Lissitzky. The descriptive content of such works became more explicit; and under the pressure of Socialist Realism, enshrined as the official art of the Soviet Union in 1934, the experimental flame that had inspired Russian avant-garde art was finally extinguished.

I should like to express my gratitude to my husband Martin Hammer for his help and advice in writing this essay. CL

CHRISTINA LODDER

NOTES

1   See the list of exhibits for the First and Second Golden Fleece exhibitions April-May 1908 and January-February 1909 in Donald E. Gordon, *Modern Art Exhibitions 1900-1916*, Munich, 1974, Vol. 2, pp. 262-66 and 307-10.

2   See Gordon, *Modern Art Exhibitions*, Vol. 2, p. 371.

3   David Burliuk, 'Golos impressionista – v zashchitu zhivopisi' (The Voice of an Impressionist – in Defence of Painting), *Zveno* (The Link), exhibition catalogue, Kiev, 1908, from John E. Bowlt, ed., *Russian Art of the Avant-Garde; Theory and Criticism 1902-1934*, London, 1988, pp. 10-11.

4   Aleksandr Shevchenko, *Neoprimitivizm. Ego teoriya. Ego vozmozhnosti. Ego dostizheniya* (Neoprimtivism: Its Theory: Its Potentials: Its Achievements), Moscow 1913 (text dated June 1913), from Bowlt, *Russian Art*, p. 49.

5   Shevchenko, *Neoprimitivizm*, from Bowlt, *Russian Art*, p. 46.

6   Four works by Pirosmanashvili were exhibited at The Target Exhibition in Moscow in April 1913. See Gordon, *Modern Art Exhibitions*, Vol. 2, p. 709.

7   This exhibition was called Genuine Icon Painting and Lubki, and included 120 items of folk art, six Persian *lubki*, ninety Chinese *lubki* from various collections, and in addition 123 icons, 170 Russian *lubki*, seventy-six Japanese woodcuts, seventeen Tartar *lubki*, and nine French *lubki* from Larionov's collection. See Gordon, *Modern Art Exhibitions*, Vol 2, pp. 708-9.

8   See Gordon, *Modern Art Exhibitions*, Vol. 2, p. 563.

9   V. Lobanov, *Khudozhestvennye gruppirovki za poslednie 25 let* (Artistic Groupings Over The Past Twenty-Five Years), Moscow, 1930, p. 62.

10 See John E. Bowlt, 'Neo-primitivism and Russian Painting', *The Burlington Magazine*, March 1974, p. 138.

11 See Vladimir Dahl, *Tolkovyi slovar zhivago Velikoruskago yazyka*, Vol.2, Moscow, 1881, p. 99.

12 Goncharova listed five paintings of 1912 as 'Jews (primitive)' (see E. Eganburi, *Natalya Goncharova. Mikhail Larionov*, Moscow, 1913, p. XII). For other examples of this series see *Jews: Sabbath* 1912, Tartarstan Museum of Fine Arts, Kazan, reproduced in A. D. Sarab'yanov, *Neizvestnyi Russkii Avangard v muzeyakh i chastnykh sobraniyakh*, Moscow, 1992, p. 73; and *Jewish Family* 1912, Private Collection, Paris, reproduced in Mary Chamot, *Gontcharova*, Paris, 1972, p. 49.

13 Goncharova as cited by Benedikt Livshits, *Polutoraglazyi strelets* (The One-and-a-Half-Eyed Archer), Leningrad, 1933, p. 80; from Bowlt, *Russian Art*, p. 78.

14 Shchukin purchased *Dryad* in 1908 (see Beverly Whitney Kean, *All The Empty Palaces: The Merchant Patrons of Modern Art in Pre-Revolutionary Russia*, London, 1983, pp. 166-8).

15 Kandinsky, 'Reminiscences' (1913) in Kenneth Lindsay and Peter Vergo, eds., *Kandinsky. Complete Writings on Art*, London, 1982, Vol 1, p. 373.

16 Kandinsky, 'On the Spiritual in Art' (1912) in *Kandinsky: Complete Writings on Art*, Vol. 1, pp. 127-219.

17 Larionov and Goncharova, 'Luchisty i budushchniki. Manifest' (Rayists and Futurists: A Manifesto), in *Oslinyi khvost i mishen* (Donkey's Tail and Target), Moscow, 1913, from Bowlt, *Russian Art*, p. 90.

18 *Ibid.*

19 *Ibid.*

20 It seems unlikely that Rayism emerged before 1912 since *The Head of a Soldier*, reproduced in the catalogue of the second Blaue Reiter exhibition in Munich in March 1912, only shows the beginnings of a move towards a more dynamic use of line, which would eventually culminate in Rayism. Larionov showed his first works with Rayist titles in November and December 1912. See Gordon, *Modern Art Exhibitions*, Vol 2, pp. 642 and 525. Contemporary reviews make clear that the latter exhibition of the Union of Youth was open from December 1912 to January 1913 and not 1911-12 as Gordon states.

21 Apollinaire's review of Goncharova and Larionov's exhibition appeared in *Soirées de Paris*, July 1914. See *Apollinaire on Art: Essays and Reviews 1902-1918*, London, 1972, p.413.

22 See, trans., Xenia Glowacki-Prus, ed., Troels Andersen, *K. S. Malevich: The Artist, Infinity, Suprematism: Unpublished Writings 1913-1933*, Copenhagen, 1978, p.201, notes p. 239. For a discussion of the term Cubo-Futurism see Vladimir Markov, *Russian Futurism: A History*, London, 1968, pp. 117-9.

23 See *L'Avant-Garde Russe: Chefs-d'Oeuvre des Musées Russe 1905-1925*, Musée des Beaux-Arts de Nantes, 1993, p. 184.

24 This painting is almost identical to *Portrait 1914-15* (Costakis Collection) reproduced in Angelica Rudenstein, ed., *Russian Avant-Garde Art: The George Costakis Collection*, London, 1981, p. 363. The difference is that the Costakis version does not include collage elements. Both works are related to a whole series of portraits which Popova executed in 1914-15 in this manner (see Magdalena Dabrowski, *Liubov Popova*, Museum of Modern Art, New York, 1991, pp. 50-53).

25 Catalogue of Union of Youth Exhibition, 23 November 1913 – 23 January 1914, in Gordon, *Modern Art Exhibitions*, Vol. 2, p. 768.

26 Kazimir Malevich, *Ot kubizma i futurizma do suprematizma. Novy zhivopisny realizm* (From Cubism and Futurism to Suprematism; The New Realism in Painting), Moscow, 1915, third edition 1916 in trans., Xenia Glowacki-Prus and Arnold McMillin, ed., Troels Andersen, *K.S. Malevich: Essays on Art 1915-1933*, London, 1971, Vol. 1, pp. 19-41. All of the quotations in this paragraph are taken from this text.

27 *Poslednaya futuristicheskaya vystavka kartin 0.10 (nul desyat)* (Last Futurist Exhibition of Paintings 0.10 [Zero Ten]) reproduced in Herman Berninger and Jean-Albert Cartier, *Jean Pougny*, Tübingen, 1972, Vol. 1, pp. 58-9.

28 See Mikhail Matyushin, 'O knige Metzanzhe-Gleza "Du Cubisme"' (Concerning the book of Gleizes and Metzinger *Du Cubisme*), *Soyuz Molodezhi* (Union of Youth), No. 3, 1913, pp. 25-34. For an English translation see Linda Dalrymple Henderson, *The Fourth Dimension and Non-Euclidean Geometry in Modern Art*, Princeton, 1983, pp. 368-375.

29 Malevich, letter to Alexandre Benois, May 1916, in K. Malevich, *Ecrits II: Le Miroir Suprématiste*, Lausanne, 1977, p. 33.

30 El Lissitzky and Hans Arp, *Die Kunstismen 1914-1924*, Zurich/Munich/Leipzig, 1925, p. xi.

31 See Nikolai Punin, *Pamyatnik tretego internatsionala* (Monument to the Third International), Petrograd, 1920 and Tatlin's declaration 'Nasha predstoyashchaya rabota' (The Work Ahead of Us), *VIII sezd sovetov (Ezhednevnyi byulleten s'ezda VTsIK)* (Eighth Congress of the Soviets: Daily Bulletin of the Congress VTsIK) No. 13, 1 January 1921, in Bowlt, *Russian Art*, p. 207.

32 *Ibid.*

33 See 'Programme of the Working Group of Constructivists' in Selim O. Khan-Magomedov, *Rodchenko: The Complete Work*, London, 1986, pp. 289-90.

34 Osip Brik, 'Ot kartiny k sittsu' (From Pictures to Textile Prints), *LEF*, No. 2, 1924, author's translation. The text is given in full in Bowlt, ed., *Russian Art*, pp. 244-9.

35 Varvara Stepanova, 'O polozhenii i zadachakh khudozhnika-konstruktivista v sittsenabivnoi promyshlennosti v svyazi s rabotami na sittsenabivnoi fabrike' (Concerning the position and tasks of the artist-constructor in the textile printing industry, in connection with work at a textile printing factory), cited by Christina Lodder, *Russian Constructivism*, London and Newhaven, 1983, p.151.

COLOUR PLATES

1 **LARIONOV**
A WOMAN PASSING BY
1909, cat. no. 38

2 **LARIONOV**
SOLDIER IN A WOOD
c.1911, cat. no. 42

3 **LARIONOV**
THE KATSAPSKAYA VENUS
1912, cat. no. 43

4 **GONCHAROVA**
SUNFLOWERS
c.1910, cat. no. 14

5 **GONCHAROVA**
RABBI WITH CAT
1912, cat. no. 17

6 **GONCHAROVA**
A PROVINCIAL LANDSCAPE
1909-10, cat. no. 12

7 **GONCHAROVA**
MOSCOW WINTER
1910-11, cat. no. 15

8 **KANDINSKY**
CUPOLAS (Destiny: The Red Wall)
1909, cat. no. 23

9 **KANDINSKY**
IMPROVISATION 4
1909, cat. no. 24

10 **LENTULOV**
LANDSCAPE WITH A RED HOUSE
1917, cat. no. 50

11 **MORGUNOV**
THE BUTCHER'S SHOP
1910-11, cat. no. 62

12 **FILONOV**
THE THREE AT TABLE
1914-15, cat. no. 11

13 **FALK**
STILL LIFE: FLOWERS
1915, cat. no. 8

14 **CHAGALL**
THE POET RECLINING
1915, cat. no. 3

15 **KONCHALOVSKII**
SCHÉRHÉRAZADE
1917, cat. no. 34

16 **MALEVICH**
THE SCYTHER
1912, cat. no. 53

17 **MALEVICH**
THE REAPING WOMAN
1912, cat. no. 52

18 **EXTER**
A BANK OF THE SEINE
c.1912, cat. no. 6

19 **SHEVCHENKO**
THE MUSICIANS
1913, cat. no. 89

20 **ROZANOVA**
CITY LANDSCAPE (The City)
1913, cat. no. 81

21 **LE DANTYU**
PORTRAIT OF FABBRI
1912, cat. no. 48

22 **SHAPOSHNIKOV**
COMPOSITION WITH BLUE STRUCTURES
1918, cat. no. 88

23 **POPOVA**
CUBIST NUDE
c.1913, cat. no. 65

24 **KLYUN**
SELF PORTRAIT WITH SAW
1914, cat. no. 28

25 **POPOVA**
FUTURIST PORTRAIT
1914-15, cat. no. 66

26 **ROZANOVA**
THE QUEEN OF DIAMONDS
c.1915, cat. no. 83

27 **ROZANOVA**
THE KNAVE OF CLUBS
1915-16, cat. no. 84

28 **ROZANOVA**
CLOCK AND CARDS (The Gambler's Dream)
c.1915, cat. no. 85

29 **PESTEL**
STILL LIFE
1915, cat. no. 64

30 **UDALTSOVA**
STILL LIFE
1916, cat. no. 99

31 **MENKOV**
SYMPHONY (Violin)
1918, cat. no. 61

32 **MALEVICH**
SUPREMATISM
1916, cat. no. 54

33 **MALEVICH**
STUDY: SUPREMATIST COMPOSITION
c.1920, cat. no. 55

34 **POPOVA**
PICTORIAL ARCHITECTONICS
1916, cat. no. 68

35 **RODCHENKO**
COMPOSITION (Overcoming Red)
1918, cat. no. 78

36 **VESNIN**
STUDY OF PLANES
1917, cat. no. 100

37 **KLYUN**
SUPREMATISM
1916-18, cat. no. 30

38 **ADLIVANKIN**
STILL LIFE
1920, cat. no. 1

39 **RODCHENKO**
NON-OBJECTIVE COMPOSITION
1917, cat. no. 74

40 **POPOVA**
PICTORIAL ARCHITECTONICS
1918, cat. no. 69

41 **DEINEKO**
SUPREMATIST COMPOSITION
before 1921, cat. no. 4

42 **DYMSHITS-TOLSTAYA**
COMPOSITION OF A COMPASS
1919, cat. no. 5

43 **STRZEMINSKI**
THE METER
1919, cat. no. 97

44 **STEPANOVA**
COMPOSITION WITH RED
1920, cat. no. 95

45 **KANDINSKY**
SOUTHERN
1917, cat. no. 25

46 **MALEVICH**
THE CARPENTER
1928-32, cat. no. 58

47 **MALEVICH**
HEAD
1928-32, cat. no. 57

48 **SHTERENBERG**
A PIKE
1920s, cat. no. 92

2 LARIONOV
SOLDIER IN A WOOD
*c.*1911, cat. no. 42

3 LARIONOV
THE KATSAPSKAYA VENUS
1912, cat. no. 43

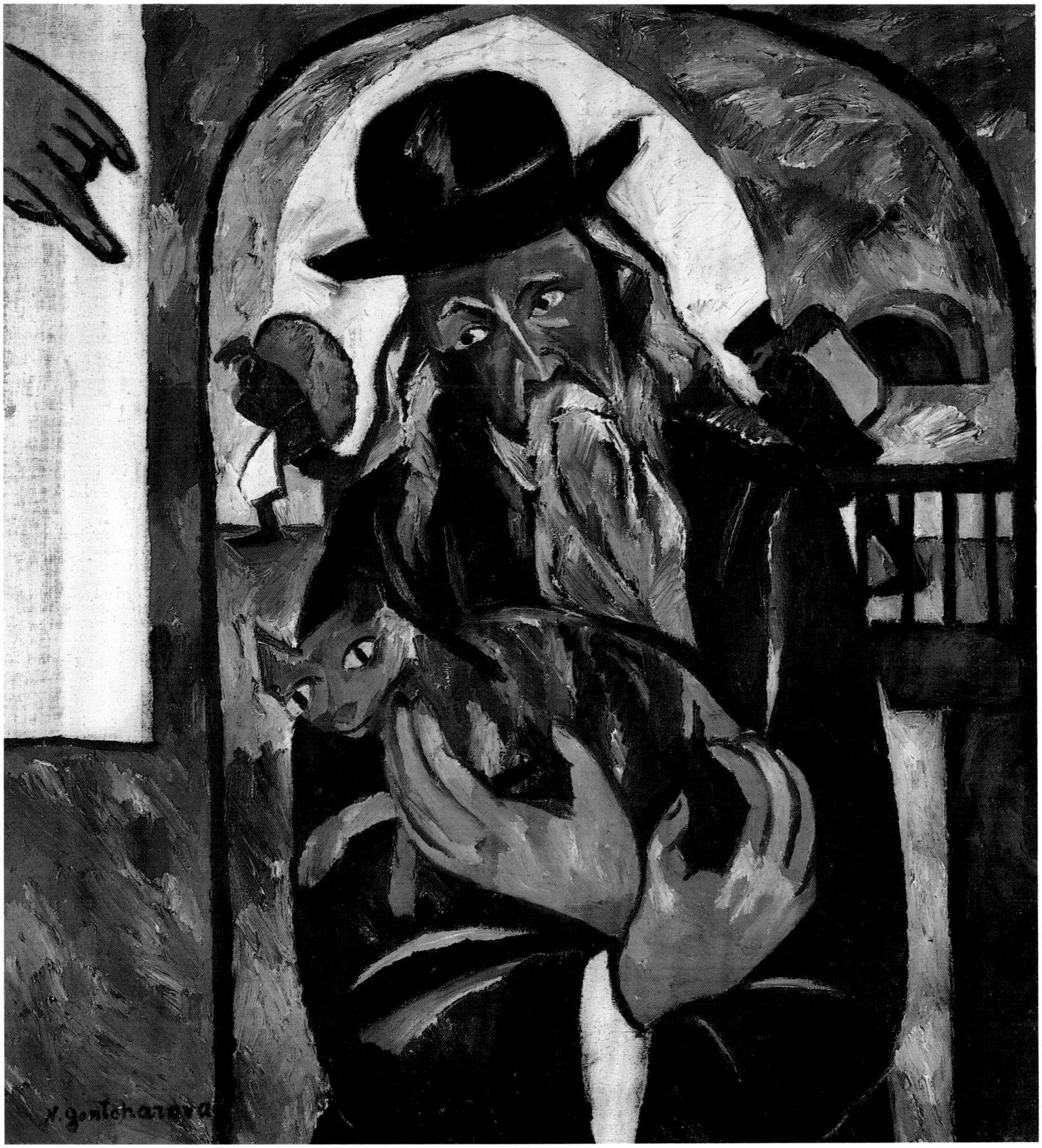

5 GONCHAROVA
RABBI WITH CAT
1912, cat. no. 17

7 GONCHAROVA
MOSCOW WINTER
1910–11, cat. no. 15

8 KANDINSKY
CUPOLAS (Destiny: The Red Wall)
1909, cat. no. 23

11 MORGUNOV
THE BUTCHER'S SHOP
1910–11, cat. no. 62

13 FALK
STILL LIFE: FLOWERS
1915, cat. no. 8

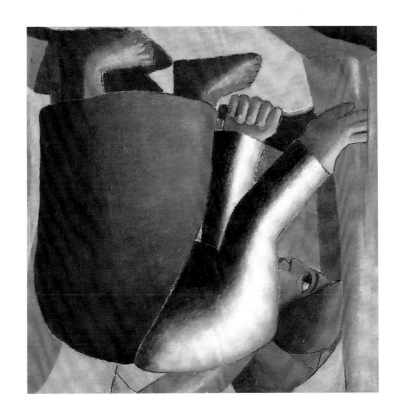

165

18 EXTER
A BANK OF THE SEINE
*c.*1912, cat. no. 6

19 SHEVCHENKO
THE MUSICIANS
1913, cat. no. 89

21 LE DANTYU
PORTRAIT OF FABBRI
1912, cat. no. 48

22 SHAPOSHNIKOV
COMPOSITION WITH BLUE STRUCTURES
1918, cat. no. 88

23 POPOVA
CUBIST NUDE
c1913, cat. no. 65

24 KLYUN
SELF PORTRAIT WITH SAW
1914, cat. no. 28

25 POPOVA
FUTURIST PORTRAIT
1914–15, cat. no. 66

26 ROZANOVA
THE QUEEN OF DIAMONDS
*c.*1915, cat. no. 83

27 ROZANOVA
THE KNAVE OF CLUBS
1915–16, cat. no. 84

28 ROZANOVA
CLOCK AND CARDS (The Gambler's Dream)
c.1915, cat. no. 85

30 UDALTSOVA
STILL LIFE
1916, cat. no. 99

31 MENKOV
SYMPHONY (Violin)
1918, cat. no. 61

32 MALEVICH
SUPREMATISM
1916, cat. no. 54

33 MALEVICH
STUDY: SUPREMATIST COMPOSITION
*c.*1920, cat. no. 55

39 RODCHENKO
NON-OBJECTIVE COMPOSITION
1917, cat. no. 74

40 POPOVA
PICTORIAL ARCHITECTONICS
1918, cat. no. 69

41 DEINEKO
SUPREMATIST COMPOSITION
before 1921, cat. no. 4

42 DYMSHITS-TOLSTAYA
COMPOSITION OF A COMPASS
1919, cat. no. 5

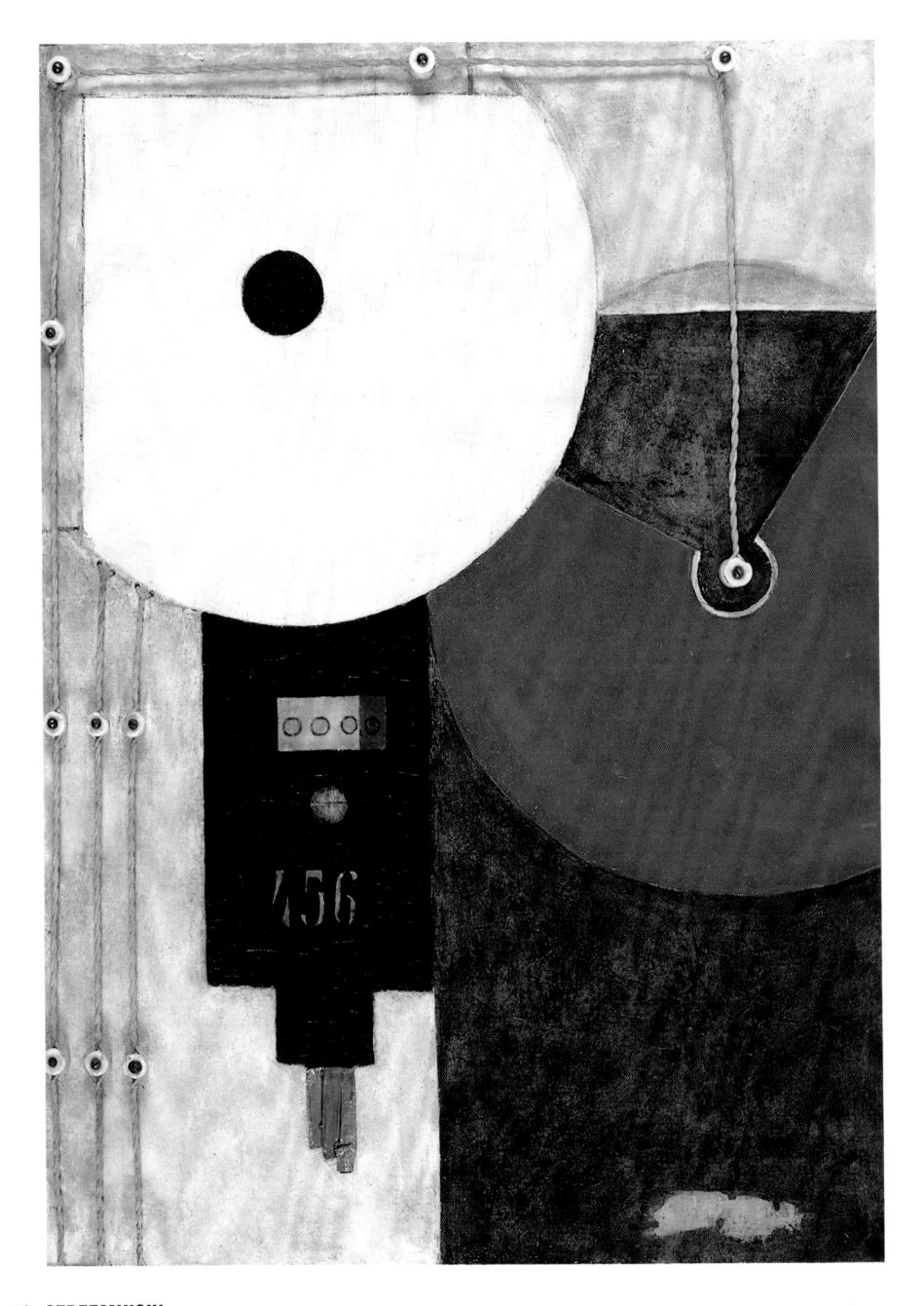

43 STRZEMINSKI
THE METER
1919, cat. no. 97

44 STEPANOVA
COMPOSITION WITH RED
1920, cat. no. 95

46 MALEVICH
THE CARPENTER
1928-32, cat. no. 58

48 SHTERENBERG
A PIKE
1920s, cat. no. 92

CATALOGUE

An asterisk indicates that the work is illustrated
in colour between pages 25 and 72.

SAMUIL ADLIVANKIN 1897-1966

Born in Tatarsk, Adlivankin received his initial artistic training in Odessa (1912-17), later moving to Moscow where he studied at the State Free Art Studios with Vladimir Tatlin (1918-19). As a member of IZO he was responsible for organising Free Art Studios in Samara and Ekaterinburg. At this time he explored the ideas of Cubism and Futurism, constructed counter-reliefs, and produced completely non-objective paintings. In 1921, however, he rejected all experimentation in favour of figuration, becoming a founder member of NOZh, the New Society of Painters.

1* STILL LIFE 1920
[colour plate 38] oil on wood, 52.5 x 41 cm
Art Museum, Yaroslavl

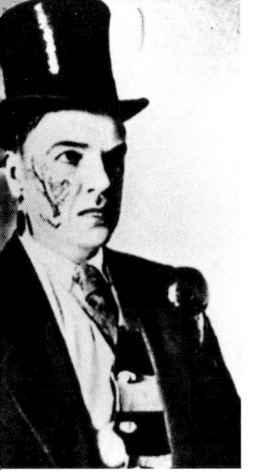

David Burliuk, 1913

Marc Chagall with wife and child, 1917

DAVID BURLIUK 1882-1967

Burliuk studied in Kazan, Odessa and Moscow (1898-9, 1899-1900, 1911-14) and also in Munich (1902-3) and Paris (1904). He became one of the leading figures of the Russian avant-garde from 1908 onwards, organising groups, exhibitions and debates, and publishing manifestos, essays and numerous illustrated Futurist books. Initially, Burliuk painted in a Post-Impressionist style, but around 1910, and possibly under the influence of Larionov, he embraced Neoprimitivism. Burliuk participated in the first exhibition of Der Blaue Reiter in Munich (1911-12) and contributed to the group's publication with an article on 'The "Savages" of Russia'. In 1912-13 he published the celebrated manifesto *A Slap in the Face of Public Taste* with the poets Aleksei Kruchenykh, Vladimir Mayakovskii and Velimir Khlebnikov in the book of the same name. This publication, which contained Burliuk's essays on Cubism and *faktura* (texture), was the mouthpiece of the Futurist group of poets, Hylea, which he organised. In 1913 Mayakovskii, Vasilii Kamenskii and Burliuk visited seventeen Russian cities, presenting a series of outrageous Futurist perfomances. Burliuk left Moscow in 1915, living in the Urals (1915-17) and Japan (1920-22) before finally settling in the United States in 1922.

2 BULLS 1907-08
oil on canvas, 58 x 70 cm
Regional Art Museum, Samara

MARC CHAGALL 1887-1985

Having trained in Vitebsk and St Petersburg (1906-9), Chagall studied in Paris at l'Académie la Palette and l'Académie de la Grande Chaumière (1910-14). In Paris, Chagall explored the possibilities of Cubism but frequently applied its principles to Jewish subject-matter, producing paintings which had much in common with Russian Neoprimitivism. In Russia between 1914 and 1922 he became an important figure in the Jewish artistic movement, illustrating books and executing decorations for the Yiddish theatre in Vitebsk and Moscow (1920-1). In charge of art in Vitebsk in 1918, Chagall founded the Vitebsk Art School (1919) from which he was ousted in 1920 by

Malevich whom he himself had invited to come as a teacher. In 1921 he left Moscow, eventually settling permanently in France in 1922.

3* THE POET RECLINING 1915
[colour plate 14]
oil on millboard, 77 x 77.5 cm
The Trustees of the Tate Gallery, London

OLGA DEINEKO 1897-1970

Having studied privately in St Petersburg, Deineko attended the VKhUTEMAS in Moscow (1919-23) where she came under the influence of the latest artistic ideas, including Suprematism. During the 1920s she specialised in illustrating children's books and was subsequently active in poster design.

4* SUPREMATIST COMPOSITION before 1921
[colour plate 41]
oil and tempera on canvas, 45 x 50.5 cm
Regional Art Museum, Tula

SOFYA DYMSHITS-TOLSTAYA
1889-1963

Dymshits-Tolstaya studied in St. Petersburg (1906-10) and Paris (1910-11). She was close to Tatlin and under his direction she apparently wrote the text for the brochure *Vladimir Evgrafovich Tatlin* published in 1915. She started working directly with materials from *c*.1916 onwards, exploring various textures in her paintings by applying alien elements onto the canvas, producing collages and constructing reliefs from wood, metal and glass. Her most innovative works are abstract constructions assembled from layers of glass, some of which were painted. Between 1918 and 1921 she worked for IZO and from the mid-1920s onwards she was active in publishing, designing layouts for the journals *The Working Woman* and *Peasant Woman*, and producing posters.

5* COMPOSITION OF A COMPASS 1919
[colour plate 42]
oil, sand, aluminium paint and cord on canvas,
69 x 53 cm
Regional Art Museum, Samara

Sofya Dymshits-Tolstaya

ALEXANDRA EXTER 1882-1949

Exter (of Greek origin) studied in Kiev (1901-3, 1906-8) and at l'Académie de la Grande Chaumière, Paris (1908). From 1908 she spent at least half of her time in Paris, where she had a studio, and became acquainted with the leading representatives of Cubism and Futurism: Picasso, Braque, Delaunay, Soffici and Marinetti. Her paintings reflect her direct knowledge of these movements and some canvases possess particularly strong affinities with the work of Delaunay. Exter exhibited frequently with the Russian avant-garde from 1908 and acted as a first-hand source of information concerning Western developments. In 1915-16 she started to produce abstract paintings consisting of dynamic configurations of boldly coloured planar elements. During the Civil War she painted revolutionary decorations and agitational trains (1919). She taught in Odessa and Kiev (1918-20) and at the Moscow VKhUTEMAS (1921-2). She became associated with Constructivism in 1921, and produced theatrical, clothing and film designs before settling in France in 1924.

6* A BANK OF THE SEINE *c*.1912
[colour plate 18] oil on canvas, 80.5 x 64.5 cm
Art Museum, Yaroslavl

7 COMPOSITION: THE MOVEMENT OF PLANES *c*.1917
oil on canvas, 93 x 76 cm
State Museum of Fine Arts, Nizhnii Tagil

ROBERT FALK 1886-1958

Falk studied intermittently at the Moscow School of
Painting, Sculpture and Architecture (1905-12) and in
1910 was one of the founder members of the Knave of
Diamonds group. In 1913, having experimented with
pointillism and produced some lyrical Neoprimitivist
canvases, Falk began a more intensive assimilation of
Cézanne's work with a freedom which indicates the
strong influence of Braque and Picasso's early Cubist
paintings. Falk continued to work in this style,
although by the early 1920s he had (in his own words)
adopted a 'more realistic position'. He worked in IZO
(1918-20), taught at the State Free Art Studios and the
VKhUTEMAS (1918-28).

8* STILL LIFE: FLOWERS 1915
[colour plate 13] oil on canvas, 85.5. x 70 cm
B.M. Kustodiev Art Gallery, Astrakhan

9 A VILLAGE IN THE CRIMEA 1915
oil on canvas, 125 x 81 cm
State Russian Museum, St Petersburg

PAVEL FILONOV 1883-1941

Filonov studied in St Petersburg (1897-1910), becoming an
active member of the Union of Youth (1910-14) and
close to the Hylea group of poets (Vladimir
Mayakovskii, the Burliuk brothers, Velimir Khlebnikov
and Aleksei Kruchenykh). He illustrated Futurist
books (eg Khlebnikov's *Selected Poems*, 1911) and in
1915 published his own neologist book *Chant of
Universal Flowering*. From 1912
he started formulating his theory
of analytical art and the concept
of the 'made' painting. He
initially worked in a highly
detailed, essentially
Neoprimitivist style with strong
overtones of German
Expressionism (1910-13). On to
this he grafted certain Cubist
devices such as faceting and
spatial dislocation which were
used to intensify the psycho-

Pavel Filonov and wife, 1930s

logical structure of the image and evoke the notion of
growth and transformation. During World War I he
fought on the Rumanian front (1916-18) and became
head of the local revolutionary military committee. In
1923 he published his declaration of 'World Flowering'
and propagated his ideas through his teaching at the
Academy of Arts in Petrograd where he formed his
own group called The Masters of Analytical Art.

10 MAN AND WOMAN 1912-13
oil on paper laid down on canvas, 154 x 123 cm
State Russian Museum, St. Petersburg

11* THE THREE AT TABLE 1914-15
[colour plate 12] oil on canvas, 100 x 102 cm
State Russian Museum, St. Petersburg

NATALYA GONCHAROVA 1881-1962

Goncharova studied at the Moscow School of Painting,
Sculpture and Architecture (1898-1909) where she
met Larionov in 1900, with whom she collaborated and
lived for the rest of her life. Together they led the
avant-garde from 1908 to 1914. From 1906 onwards
she began to experiment with the ideas of Post-
Impressionism, Cézanne, Fauvism and eventually early
Cubism, developing an independent style of
Neoprimitivism which fused Western ideas with native
sources of inspiration, notably the icon and the *lubok*.
In 1912 she began to explore more advanced ideas of
Cubism and Futurism which led her and Larionov to
develop Rayism. She exhibited briefly with the Knave
of Diamonds (1910-11) and Union of Youth (1910),
working alongside Larionov at the Donkey's Tail (1912)
and Target (1913) exhibitions. She illustrated
numerous Futurist books in various styles (eg *Game
in Hell*, *The World Backwards, Hermits*) and designed
stage sets (eg *The Golden Cockerel* for Diaghilev,
1914). In 1915, at Diaghilev's invitation, she and
Larionov left Moscow, settling in Paris in 1917.

12* A PROVINCIAL LANDSCAPE 1909-10
[colour plate 6] oil on canvas, 70 x 70 cm
State Russian Museum, St Petersburg

13 STILL LIFE WITH GREEN BOTTLE 1909-10
oil on canvas, 72.5 x 82.5 cm
Regional Art Museum, Simbirsk

14* SUNFLOWERS *c.*1910
[colour plate 4] oil on canvas, 100 x 93 cm
State Russian Museum, St Petersburg

15* MOSCOW WINTER 1910-11
[colour plate 7] oil on canvas, 99 x 106 cm
Regional Art Museum, Simbirsk

16 HOAR-FROST 1911
oil on canvas, 118 x 99 cm
State Russian Museum, St Petersburg

17* RABBI WITH CAT 1912
[colour plate 5] oil on canvas, 100.2 x 92 cm
Scottish National Gallery of Modern Art, Edinburgh

18 PEASANTS PICKING GRAPES 1912
oil on canvas, 145 x 130 cm
State Museum of Bashkir, Ufa

19 ORCHIDS 1913-14
oil on canvas, 93 x 71 cm
State Art Museum, Nizhnii Novgorod

20 BACKDROP DESIGN FOR 'LE COQ D'OR' ACT II
1913-14
watercolour on paper, 65.8 x 99.6 cm
Scottish National Gallery of Modern Art, Edinburgh

21 THE FOREST *c.*1913
oil on canvas, 53.8 x 81 cm
Scottish National Gallery of Modern Art, Edinburgh

22 COSTUME DESIGN FOR ONE OF THE THREE
KINGS IN 'LA LITURGIE' 1915
watercolour over pencil with collage, 62.2 x 47.6 cm
Scottish National Gallery of Modern Art, Edinburgh

Wassily Kandinsky, Munich *c.*1913

WASSILY KANDINSKY 1866-1944

After a career in law which included an expedition to study the customs and arts of the primitive peoples in the Vologda region of Russia (1889), Kandinsky moved to Munich in 1896 to study painting. Between 1910 and 1911 he completed his treatise *Concerning the Spiritual in Art* and started experimenting with abstraction. Although his earliest paintings were inspired by Russian folk art, he gradually eliminated most representational forms from his pictures, creating non-objective compositions in saturated colours, often on the analogy of musical compositions. He was instrumental in publishing *Der Blaue Reiter* and organising the group's two exhibitions, which reflect his continued contacts with Russia. Returning to Moscow after the outbreak of the First World War, he became active in artistic life, working for the purchasing commission of IZO, teaching at the State Free Art Studios, and founding INKhUK in 1920 for which he formulated a research programme. Kandinsky returned to Germany in 1921 and joined the staff of the Bauhaus. After the Nazi advent to power in 1933, he settled in France.

23* CUPOLAS (DESTINY: THE RED WALL) 1909
[colour plate 8] oil on canvas, 85 x 116 cm
B. M. Kustodiev Art Gallery, Astrakhan
No. 264 in Hans K. Roethel and Jean K. Benjamin,
Kandinsky: Catalogue Raisonné of the Oil Paintings,
2 vols, London, 1982 and 1984, as *Cupolas*.

24* IMPROVISATION 4 1909
[colour plate 9] oil on canvas, 107 x 158 cm
State Art Museum, Nizhnii Novgorod
No. 282 in *Catalogue Raisonné*.

25* SOUTHERN 1917
[colour plate 45] oil on canvas 73 x 102 cm
B.M. Kustodiev Art Gallery, Astrakhan
No. 618 in *Catalogue Raisonné* as location unknown
and not illustrated.

26 MUSICAL OVERTURE: THE VIOLET WEDGE
1919
oil on canvas, 59 x 68 cm
Regional Art Museum, Tula
No. 662 in *Catalogue Raisonné* as *The Violet Wedge*
and location unknown.

Ivan Klyun, *c*.1915

IVAN KLYUN 1873-1934

Klyun trained in Kiev, Warsaw and Moscow. He met
Malevich in 1907 and remained close to him artistically
until *c*.1920. Klyun experimented with Cubism and
Futurism (1912-15) and started making reliefs in 1914.
From 1913 he contributed to all the major avant-garde
exhibitions, publishing his manifesto at 0.10 (Zero Ten)
in 1915. Klyun belonged to Supremus and painted in a
Suprematist style from 1915-19, thereafter adopting a
more individual abstract idiom. He designed
decorations for the May Day celebrations (1918),
taught at the State Free Art Studios and the
VKhUTEMAS (1918-21) and was a member of INKhUK. He
continued to paint abstract works until the mid-1920s
when he adopted the Purist style of Ozenfant, joining
OST in 1925.

27 LIFE IN THE GRAND HOTEL 1913-14
oil on canvas, 108 x 71 cm
Regional Art Museum, Samara
Traditionally ascribed to Malevich but now thought to
be by Klyun.

28* SELF PORTRAIT WITH SAW 1914
[colour plate 24] oil on canvas, 71 x 62 cm
B. M. Kustodiev Art Gallery, Astrakhan

29 UNTITLED 1916
oil paint and wood on wooden board,
37.5 x 17.5 x 7 cm
Annely Juda Fine Art, London

30* SUPREMATISM 1916-18
[colour plate 37] oil on canvas, 49 x 44 cm
Art Museum, Yaroslavl

31 NON-OBJECTIVE COMPOSITION 1921
oil on canvas, 49 x 55.5 cm
Rossizo, Moscow

32 UNTITLED 1922
oil on carpet, 52.5 x 54 cm
Annely Juda Fine Art, London

PETR KONCHALOVSKII 1876-1956

Konchalovskii trained at the Académie Julian, Paris (1897-
8), and in St Petersburg (1899-1905). He travelled
fairly extensively, visiting Spain (1910), Germany and
Italy (1912) and Paris (1913). He was a founder member
of the Knave of Diamonds (1910-16) and between 1908
and 1913 his painting reflected the influence of French
developments such as Fauvism, Cézannism and
Cubism. After the Revolution, he taught at the State
Free Art Studios and at the VKhUTEMAS (1918-29).

33 CIGARS AND SOMBRERO 1916
oil on canvas, 71 x 58 cm
State Russian Museum, St. Petersburg

34* SCHÉRHÉRAZADE 1917
[colour plate 15] oil on canvas, 108 x 142 cm
Regional Art Museum, Tula

ALEKSEI KRAVCHENKO 1889-1940

Kravchenko studied intermittently in Moscow (1904-10) and
also in Munich with Hollosy (1905-6). He travelled to
Italy, Greece and Turkey (1910) and to India and
Ceylon (1913-14). His paintings, produced within a
somewhat lyrical Neoprimitivist idiom, reflect his
interest in early Cubism. Kravchenko lived in Saratov
(1918-21) where he taught and ran the Art Museum.
He also worked extensively in linocuts, engraving and
etching.

35 PINK HOUSE BY A RIVER 1920s
oil on canvas board, 44.5 x 55 cm
Regional Art Museum, Samara

ALEKSANDR KUPRIN 1880-1960

Kuprin studied in Voronezh (1896-1901), St Petersburg (1902-4) and Moscow (1904-10), also visiting Italy and France (1913-14). He was an active member of the Knave of Diamonds group (1910-16). His paintings of the mid-1910s were boldy coloured and strongly influenced by Cézanne and Fauvism, with some Cubist elements. He produced decorations for the revolutionary festivals (1918-20) and taught at the State Free Art Studios in Moscow and Nizhnii Novgorod (1920-22) and later at the Moscow VKhUTEMAS (1922-5). In the 1920s he adopted a more realistic style.

36 STILL LIFE 1920s
verso: *Still Life* 1919
oil on canvas, 128 x 144 cm
Regional Art Museum, Tula

MIKHAIL LARIONOV 1881-1964

Larionov studied at the Moscow School of Painting, Sculpture and Architecture (1898-1908) where he met Goncharova, his lifelong companion. In autumn 1906, he encountered paintings by Gauguin and the Fauves in Paris and by Turner in London. He subsequently abandoned Impressionism and assimilated these stimuli, becoming one of the leaders of the Russian avant-garde from 1907 until World War I. During his various periods of military service (winter 1910 – summer 1911, spring 1912 and spring 1913) Larionov produced paintings on soldier themes. In 1910 he helped to organise the Knave of Diamonds group, but he left it in 1911 because he considered it too 'Cézannist'. Committed to creating a Russian art on the basis of vernacular sources, he arranged the Donkey's Tail Exhibition (1912) where he showed over thirty Neoprimitivist paintings. He exhibited his first Rayist works in November and December 1912, and published his manifesto *Rayism* in April the following year. In 1915, having been wounded, he left Russia for Switzerland to work with Diaghilev on theatrical design. In 1917 he settled in Paris.

37 LANDSCAPE 1909-10
oil on canvas, 71 x 55 cm
State Art Museum, Nizhnii Novgorod

Vladimir Lebedev, early 1920s

38* A WOMAN PASSING BY 1909
[colour plate 1] oil on canvas, 93 x 78 cm
Regional Art Museum, Simbirsk

39 A BRAWL IN THE TAVERN (AT THE INN)
1909-10
oil on canvas, 70.7 x 93.6 cm
State Art Museum, Nizhnii Novgorod

40 PEACOCK 1910
oil on canvas, 103.5 x 98 cm
Regional Art Museum, Simbirsk

41 THE CAMP 1910 -11
oil on canvas, 72 x 89.6 cm
State Russian Museum, St. Petersburg

42* SOLDIER IN A WOOD *c.*1911
[colour plate 2] oil on canvas, 84.5 x 91.4 cm
Scottish National Gallery of Modern Art, Edinburgh

43* THE KATSAPSKAYA VENUS
or THE SQUADDY'S VENUS 1912
[colour plate 3] oil on canvas, 99.5 x 129.5 cm
State Art Museum, Nizhnii Novgorod

44 THE SEA 1912-13
oil on canvas, 50 x 70.5 cm
State Art Museum, Nizhnii Novgorod

45 COSTUME DESIGN FOR 'LES CONTES RUSSES'
1915
watercolour and pencil on paper, 63.4 x 43.7 cm
Scottish National Gallery of Modern Art, Edinburgh

VLADIMIR LEBEDEV 1891-1967

Trained in St Petersburg (1910-16), Lebedev produced paintings inspired by Cubism and Futurism, as well as totally abstract canvases and reliefs. He taught at the State Free Art Studios in Moscow (1918-21) and also designed stencilled posters for the Russian Telegraphic Agency (ROSTA) in Petrograd (1920-21). During the 1920s and 1930s he continued to work extensively as a graphic artist, illustrating children's books and official publications.

46* GERANIUM 1919
[colour illustration on back cover]
verso: *Still Life with Umbrella* before 1919
oil on canvas, 67 x 57.5 cm
Art Museum, Yaroslavl

MIKHAIL LE DANTYU 1891-1917

While studying at the Academy in St Petersburg (1909-12), Le Dantyu joined the Union of Youth (1910-11). He also became close friends with the artist-poets Kirill and Ilya Zdanevich. In 1912 he moved to Moscow where he was in contact with Tatlin, Goncharova and particularly with Larionov who exerted a strong influence on him and with whom he exhibited (1912-14). Le Dantyu's paintings of the mid-1910s show the influence of Cubism, Futurism and Larionov's Rayism. Le Dantyu also developed the concept of *vsechestvo* or 'allness' which consisted of assimilating and reworking all the painting styles which existed throughout the world. While in the Caucasus visiting the Zdanevich brothers (1912-13) Le Dantyu discovered the work of the signboard painter Niko Pirosmanashvili which was subsequently celebrated by the avant-garde and exhibited at the Target exhibition (1913). Mobilised in 1915, Le Dantyu was killed in action in 1917.

47 PORTRAIT OF A WOMAN *c.*1912
oil on canvas, 104 x 63 cm
Regional Art Museum, Samara

48* PORTRAIT OF FABBRI 1912
[colour plate 21] oil on canvas, 76.5 x 65 cm
Regional Art Museum, Samara

49 PORTRAIT OF AN ACTOR 1912
oil on canvas, 67 x 52 cm
Art Museum, Yaroslavl

ARISTARKH LENTULOV 1882-1943

Lentulov studied in Penza (1898-1900, 1905-6), Kiev (1900-5) and at l'Académie la Palette in Paris with Le Fauconnier and Metzinger (1911-12). In 1910 he and Larionov set up the Knave of Diamonds group with which he continued to exhibit until 1916. Lentulov's early works display the influence of Fauvism but after 1912 his paintings are more Cubist, with brightly coloured fragments in decorative, flat arrangements. In 1914 he coined the term 'Orneism' to describe his manner of applying ornamental elements such as silver paper to the surface of the painting. A member of IZO, Lentulov also taught at the State Free Studios and the VKhUTEMAS (1919-30). In the 1920s he was active in theatrical design and mural painting, joining AKhRR in 1926.

50* LANDSCAPE WITH A RED HOUSE 1917
[colour plate 10] oil on canvas, 103 x 98 cm
Regional Art Museum, Samara

EL LISSITZKY 1890-1941

Having initially trained as an engineer in Darmstadt (1909-14), Lissitzky became involved with the Jewish artistic movement after the Revolution and illustrated numerous books on Jewish themes. While teaching at the Art School in Vitebsk in 1919 he came under the influence of Malevich and Suprematism. As a result, he developed the concept of the PROUN (Project for the Affirmation of the New) as 'an interchange station between painting and architecture', and under this title produced completely abstract paintings in which he explored some of the spatial possibilities of the vocabulary of Suprematism. In 1921 he moved to Germany where he published the magazine *Object*, worked extensively promoting Russian achievements and became an important member of the European avant-garde. From 1925 onwards he worked on photomontage, exhibition design, typographical layouts and poster design.

51 PROUN. THE 1st KESTNER PORTFOLIO 1923
6 lithographs, five 60 x 44 cm, one 44 x 60 cm
Scottish National Gallery of Modern Art, Edinburgh

KAZIMIR MALEVICH 1878-1935

Born in Kiev, Malevich studied there (1894-6) and in
Moscow. After experimenting with Impressionism,
Post-Impressionism and Symbolism, he started
working in the idiom of Neoprimitivism under the
influence of Goncharova and Larionov. Malevich
subsequently experimented with Cubism and
Futurism, developing Alogism or 'transrational'
painting in which unrelated objects are juxtaposed at
different scales (eg *An Englishman in Moscow* 1914)
creating illogical images. He publicly established
Suprematism in December 1915 when he exhibited
thirty-nine totally abstract paintings at the 0.10 (Zero
Ten) exhibition. These works, consisting of coloured
geometrical planes on white grounds, evoke
sensations of movement. In 1916 Malevich organised
the Supremus group to promote his ideas. He taught
at the State Free Art Studios in Moscow (1918-19) and
then in Vitebsk (1919-22) where he founded UNOVIS
(Affirmers of the New Art) which pursued the aim of
extending his ideas into the applied arts and
architecture. In 1922 he moved to Petrograd and
continued to work on 'spatial Suprematism'. In 1927 he
visited Germany, where his book *The Non Objective
World* was published by the Bauhaus. In the final
years of his life he returned to a more figurative
subject-matter.

Kazimir Malevich at work on *Girl with a Red Pole*
(State Tretyakov Gallery) Leningrad, April 1933

52* THE REAPING WOMAN 1912
[colour plate 17] oil on canvas, 60 x 68 cm
B. M. Kustodiev Art Gallery, Astrakhan

53* THE SCYTHER 1912
[colour plate 16] oil on canvas, 113.5 x 66.5 cm
State Art Museum, Nizhnii Novgorod

54* SUPREMATISM 1916
[colour plate 32] oil on canvas, 53.5 x 53.7 cm
Regional Art Museum, Ivanovo

55* STUDY: SUPREMATIST COMPOSITION *c.*1920
[colour plate 33] oil on canvas, 70 x 48 cm
Regional Art Museum, Tula

56 SUPREMATIST COMPOSITION *c.*1920-22
oil on wood, 62 x 29.5 cm
Private Collection, courtesy Annely Juda Fine Art,
London

57* HEAD 1928-32
[colour plate 47] oil on canvas, 61 x 41 cm
State Russian Museum, St Petersburg

58* THE CARPENTER 1928-32
[colour plate 46] oil on canvas, 71 x 44 cm
State Russian Museum, St Petersburg

ILYA MASHKOV 1881-1944

Born in the region of Saratov, Mashkov studied
intermittently at the Moscow School of Painting,
Sculpture and Architecture (1900-4, 1907-8). He was a
founder member of the Knave of Diamonds in 1910.
His Neoprimitivist paintings of 1910-13 show the
impact of Fauvism, before he became more attached
to a style based pre-eminently on Cézanne with some
features adapted from early Cubism. Mashkov taught
in his own studio (1904-17), at the State Free Art
Studios and the VKhUTEMAS (1918-30). In 1924 he
joined AKhRR.

59 STILL LIFE WITH BEGONIA 1909
oil on canvas, 89 x 105 cm
State Russian Museum, St Petersburg

MIKHAIL MENKOV 1885-1921

Born in Vilnius, Menkov studied at the Moscow School of
Painting, Sculpture and Architecture (1912-14) where
he met Malevich who was an important influence on
him. After experimenting with Cubism and Futurism,
Menkov created purely abstract paintings comprising
coloured planes on white grounds which were clearly
inspired by Malevich's Suprematism. Menkov also
produced works that employ typographical signs in
conjunction with muted geometrical planes, some of
which have musical themes. At the 0.10 Exhibition
(1915) and the Tenth State Exhibition (1919) he
published manifestos which emphasise the emotional
content to be conveyed by the coloured surface of the
painting. He entered a sanatorium in 1921 and
presumably died shortly afterwards.

60   TRAM No.6 1914
oil on canvas, 82 x 51.5 cm
Regional Art Museum, Samara

61* SYMPHONY (VIOLIN) 1918
[colour plate 31] oil on canvas, 63 x 60.5 cm
Regional Art Museum, Samara

ALEKSEI MORGUNOV 1884-1935

Born and trained in Moscow, Morgunov travelled to Italy,
France and Germany (1909-10), and was particularly
influenced by the works of Cézanne. He exhibited
with the Knave of Diamonds (1910-14), Larionov (1912-
15) and the Union of Youth (1911-14). From 1910
Morgunov produced Neoprimitivist paintings which
have strong affinities with Fauvism. From 1913-14 he
was close to Malevich and his paintings reflect the
latter's experiments with Cubism, Futurism and
Alogism. He worked for IZO (1918-21). In the 1920s he
adopted a more realistic style.

62* THE BUTCHER'S SHOP 1910-11
[colour plate 11] oil on canvas, 71 x 80 cm
Art Museum, Yaroslavl

GEORGII NOSKOV 1902-?

A native of the Tver region, Noskov seems to have moved to
Petrograd in about 1921. At some point he studied with
Malevich and was a member of UNOVIS. In 1923 he
settled in Moscow where he enrolled at the VKhUTEMAS,
specialising in sculpture. Little is known about his
subsequent career as an artist.

63   COMPOSITION *c.*1921
oil on canvas, 106 x 70 cm
Art Museum, Yaroslavl

VERA PESTEL 1887-1952

Pestel studied in her native Moscow (1904-6), with Hollosy in
Munich (1909-11), and in Paris at l'Académie la Palette
with Le Fauconnier and Metzinger (1912). Painting in a
style very similar to Udaltsova, to whom she was close,
Pestel produced canvases inspired by Cubism and
Futurism (1912-14), followed by compositions based on
combinations of geometrical planes and typographical
elements (1915-16). She was a member of Supremus
(1916-17) and for a brief period painted purely non-
objective works composed of highly textured,
overlapping planes (1917-18). In 1918 she rejected
abstraction and started painting figurative works in a
lyrical manner. From 1919 onwards she was primarily
concerned with the artistic education of children.

64* STILL LIFE 1915
[colour plate 29] oil on canvas, 67 x 50 cm
State Art Museum, Nizhnii Novgorod

Vera Pestel

Lyubov Popova, early 1920s

LYUBOV POPOVA 1889-1924

Born near Moscow, Popova studied in Paris at l'Académie la Palette under Le Fauconnier and Metzinger (1912-13). Subsequently, her own paintings reflected the influence of Cubist and Futurist ideas which she had encountered there and during her second visit to Europe in 1914. From 1915 onwards, she became a prominent member of the Russian avant-garde, contributing to important exhibitions such as Tramway V and 0.10 (Zero Ten). She joined Malevich's Supremus group and in 1916 under his influence began to produce totally non-objective paintings which she described as 'Pictorial Architectonics'. These works were characterised by dynamic overlapping geometric planes and a subtle interplay of colours. She taught at the State Free Art Studios and the VKhUTEMAS (1918-24). A member of INKhUK, she had espoused Constructivst ideas by September 1921, becoming increasingly involved with theatre design (1922-3) and producing textile designs for industrial manufacture (1923-4). She died prematurely of scarlet fever caught while nursing her son.

65* CUBIST NUDE *c.*1913
[colour plate 23] oil on canvas, 92 x 64 cm
Private Collection, courtesy Annely Juda Fine Art, London

66* FUTURIST PORTRAIT 1914-15
[colour plate 25] oil on cardboard, 58.5 x 42.5 cm
Regional Art Museum, Tula

67 STILL LIFE 1915
oil and wallpaper on canvas, 54 x 36 cm
State Art Museum, Nizhnii Novgorod

68* PICTORIAL ARCHITECTONICS 1916
[colour plate 34] oil on board, 59.4 x 39.4 cm
Scottish National Gallery of Modern Art, Edinburgh

69* PICTORIAL ARCHITECTONICS 1918
[colour plate 40] oil on canvas, 58 x 53 cm
State Art Museum, Nizhnii Novgorod

70 ORANGE PICTORIAL ARCHITECTONICS 1918
oil on cardboard, 59 x 39 cm
Art Museum, Yaroslavl

71 PICTORIAL ARCHITECTONICS 1918
oil on canvas, 106 x 80 cm
Museum of Slobodsk and Kirov Region

72 SPACE-FORCE CONSTRUCTION *c.*1921
oil on wood, 77.7 x 77.7 cm
Private Collection, courtesy Annely Juda Fine Art, London

73 TEXTILE DESIGN 1924
Pencil and coloured inks on paper, 23.4 x 19.1 cm
Private Collection

ALEKSANDR RODCHENKO 1891-1956

Born in St. Petersburg, Rodchenko was one of the pioneers of Constructivism. He trained in Kazan where he met Varvara Stepanova whom he subsequently married. In 1914 he settled in Moscow, becoming acquainted with the avant-garde including Malevich, Tatlin and Popova. In late 1915 he began to make non-objective compositions using a compass and ruler and in 1918 he produced his first three-dimensional constructions.

During the Civil War he worked in the Museums' Bureau of IZO where he was responsible for distributing works to provincial museums and galleries. In 1921 he was a founder member of the First Working Group of Constructivists, and in the 1920s further developed Constructivist principles in his teaching at the VKhUTEMAS and in his work with photography, photomontage, typography, theatrical and poster design. During the 1930s he designed photographic layouts for publications celebrating Soviet achievements such as the construction of the White Sea Canal.

74* NON-OBJECTIVE COMPOSITION 1917
[colour plate 39] oil on plywood, 76 x 50.8 cm
Regional Art Museum, Ivanovo

75 TRIANGLES 1918
oil on plywood, 72 x 31 cm
The B. M. Kustodiev Art Gallery, Astrakhan

76 STUDY FOR NON-OBJECTIVE COMPOSITION No.61 1918
from the series *The Coloured Sphere of the Circle*
oil on canvas, 42 x 36 cm
Regional Art Museum, Tula

77 NON-OBJECTIVE COMPOSITION 1918
oil on canvas, 72.7 x 49.7 cm
State Art Museum, Nizhnii Novgorod

78* COMPOSITION (OVERCOMING RED) 1918
[colour plate 35] oil on canvas, 78.5 x 62 cm
Annely Juda Fine Art, London

Rodchenko wearing a worksuit of his own design, 1922

OLGA ROZANOVA 1886-1918

After studying in Moscow (1904-10), Rozanova moved to St Petersburg and became an active member of the Union of Youth group (1911-14). Her article 'The Bases of the New Creation and the Reasons Why It Is Misunderstood' (1913), published in the group's journal, represented an important contribution to current artistic debates, arguing that 'the artist must not be a passive imitator of nature, but must actively express his attitude to it'. Rozanova experimented widely, moving from a bold Neoprimitivist style which had strong affinities with Fauvism (1912-13) to a style which mixed Cubism and Futurism (1913-15). She also briefly explored the possibilites of Rayism (1913) and three-dimensional constructions (1915). In 1916 she joined Supremus and started painting completely non-objective, Suprematist works (1916-17), evolving an individual style comprising densely organised abstract forms in highly original colour combinations (1917-18). As a member of IZO, she set up numerous provincial workshops (1918). She wrote *zaum* poetry and collaborated with Aleksei Kruchenykh on the production of Futurist books (eg *War, The Universal War*). She died prematurely of diptheria.

79 THE BUILDING SITE 1913
oil on canvas, 91.5 x 110 cm
Regional Art Museum, Samara

80 THE CITY 1913
oil on canvas, 71 x 55 cm
State Art Museum, Nizhnii Novgorod

81* CITY LANDSCAPE (THE CITY) 1913
[colour plate 20] oil on metal, 71 x 71 cm
Regional Art Museum, Samara

82 FUTURIST LANDSCAPE 1913
oil and gouache on canvas, 75.5 x 53.5 cm
Private Collection, courtesy Annely Juda Fine Art, London

83* THE QUEEN OF DIAMONDS *c.*1915
from the series *Playing Cards*
[colour plate 26] oil on canvas, 84 x 69 cm
State Art Museum, Nizhnii Novogorod

84* THE KNAVE OF CLUBS 1915-16
from the series *Playing Cards*
[colour plate 27] oil on canvas, 83 x 66 cm
Regional Art Museum, Ivanovo

85* CLOCK AND CARDS (THE GAMBLER'S DREAM)
c.1915
[colour plate 28] oil on canvas, 61 x 40.5 cm
Regional Art Museum, Samara

86 NON-OBJECTIVE COMPOSITION
(FLIGHT OF AN AEROPLANE) 1916
oil on canvas, 118 x 101 cm
Regional Art Museum, Samara

BORIS SHAPOSHNIKOV 1890-1956

Born in Moscow, Shaposhnikov studied philology and
archeology before training as an artist privately and in
Rome (1913-14). He started exhibiting in 1912. He
produced works in a Cubist style and for a short time
painted abstract compositions. He worked in IZO
(1918-20) and at the State Academy of Artistic
Sciences (1921-29) where he published extensively on
problems concerning art museums. He was arrested
in the 1930s.

87 CUBIST COMPOSITION 'THE LAST
JUDGEMENT' 1915
oil on canvas, 60.5 x 40.5 cm
Regional Art Museum, Ivanovo

88* COMPOSITION WITH BLUE STRUCTURES
1918
[colour plate 22] oil on canvas, 101 x 58 cm
B. M. Kustodiev Art Gallery, Astrakhan

ALEKSANDR SHEVCHENKO 1882-1948

Born in Kharkov, Shevchenko trained in Moscow (1899-
1909) and at the Académie Julian in Paris (1905-6).
Between 1910 and 1914 he was closely associated with
Larionov, under whose influence he embraced
Neoprimitivism (1910-13), experimented with the ideas
of Cubism and Futurism (1913-14), and even briefly
produced Rayist paintings. Shevchenko's major text
was *Neoprimitivism: Its Theory: Its Possibilities: Its
Achievements* (1913). He was an active member of the
Commission for the Preservation of Monuments and
Works of Art (1918-20), and taught at the State Free
Art Studios and the VKhUTEMAS (1918-29). In 1919, at
the Twelfth State Exhibition, he issued a manifesto
with Aleksandr Grishchenko calling for a return to the
'eternal values' of easel painting. He subsequently
joined Makovets (1922-5).

89* THE MUSICIANS 1913
[colour plate 19] oil on canvas, 114 x 104.5 cm
State Russian Museum, St Petersburg

90 STILL LIFE: FRUIT 1913
oil on canvas, 86.5 x 82 cm
Regional Art Museum, Ivanovo

91 WOMAN IRONING 1920
oil on canvas, 94 x 82 cm
State Russian Museum, St Petersburg

DAVID SHTERENBERG 1881-1948

From 1906-17 Shterenberg lived in Paris where he studied
at l'Ecole des Beaux-arts (1906-12) and at l'Académie
Vitti with Van Dongen and others. In 1917 he returned
to Russia where he held various important
administrative posts under the Bolsheviks; he ran IZO
(1918-21) and the art section of the Chief
Administration for Professional Education
(Glavprofobr). He was one of the principal organisers
of both the First Russian Exhibition in Berlin in 1922
and the Russian section of the 1925 International
Exhibition of Decorative Arts in Paris. He also taught
at the VKhUTEMAS (1920-30). Shterenberg produced
figurative compositions, which were almost abstract,
being based on very elementary arrangements of
extremely simplified forms in saturated colours within
a very freely defined, flat space. Never an extreme
innovator, in 1925 he was one of the founding
members of OST or the Society of Easel Painters.

92* A PIKE 1920s
[colour plate 48] oil on canvas, 61 x 70 cm
Regional Art Museum, Ivanovo

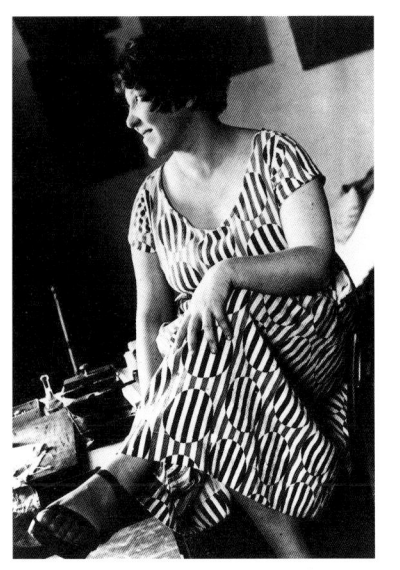

Varvara Stepanova wearing a dress of her own design (photographed by Rodchenko), c.1924

David Shterenberg, 1920s

VARVARA STEPANOVA 1894-1958

Born in Kaunas, Stepanova studied in Kazan (1910-13) where she met Rodchenko whom she later married. She moved to Moscow where she completed her training (1916-17). In 1919 she made collage books using newspaper and her own *zaum* poetry (eg *Gaust chaba* and *Rtny khomle*). She also produced a large series of paintings in which she reduced the human figure to a very simplified geometrical structure (1919-21). She worked for IZO (1918-22) and INKhUK where in 1921, along with Rodchenko and Aleksei Gan, she was responsible for organising the First Working Group of Constructivists. In the 1920s, in accordance with Constructivist principles, she worked almost exclusively in designing theatre sets, textiles, typographical layouts and posters.

95* COMPOSITION WITH RED 1920
[colour plate 44] oil on canvas, 71 x 71 cm
Regional Art Museum, Ivanovo

WŁADYSŁAW STRZEMINSKI 1893-1952

A Polish national, Strzemiński was wounded in World War I fighting for the Tsarist army (1916). He then studied with Malevich at the State Free Art Studios in Moscow (1918-19) where he experimented with avant-garde ideas including reliefs, but ultimately became closely allied with Suprematism. He worked for IZO, first in Moscow organising exhibitions (1918-19) and then in Smolensk producing propaganda posters (1920-21). He set up the Smolensk UNOVIS, but then moved to Poland where he and Katarzyna Kobro were active in developing Polish Constructivism.

96 STILL LIFE: A PLATE 1918
oil, gesso and enamel paint on canvas, laid down on wood, 29.3 x 40.3 cm
Regional Art Museum, Ivanovo

97* THE METER 1919
[colour plate 43]
oil, ceramic insulators and electric flex on canvas, laid down on wood, 81 x 58 cm
Regional Art Museum, Samara

93 STILL LIFE 1920s
oil on canvas, 56.5 x 71 cm
Regional Art Museum, Tula

NIKOLAI SINEZUBOV 1891-1948

Born in Moscow, Sinezubov trained at the Moscow School of Painting, Sculpture and Architecture (1912-17). He taught at Proletkult in 1919 and in 1920 exhibited with Kandinsky, Rodchenko and Stepanova. In the 1920s he settled in Paris.

94 LANDSCAPE: A BLUE DAY 1920
oil on canvas, 53 x 46 cm
Art Museum, Yaroslavl

VLADIMIR TATLIN 1885-1953

Tatlin trained as an artist in Moscow (1902-4) and Penza (1904-10), but his studies were interrupted by extensive trips abroad working as a sailor. He exhibited alongside Larionov and Goncharova (1910-12) and with the Union of Youth (1911-14). His early paintings were produced in a Neoprimitivist style, based on Cézanne, Fauvism, the icon and *lubok*. In 1914 he visited Paris where he met Picasso and saw his Cubist works. On his return to Russia, Tatlin began to make three-dimensional pictorial reliefs which rapidly became completely abstract. By 1915 he had begun to create more dynamic configurations, constructed in space and slung across the corners of rooms. These works established the principles of construction and *faktura* (material texture) which formed the essential basis for the emergence of Russian Constructivism in 1921. As the head of the Moscow IZO, Tatlin was responsible for implementing Lenin's Plan for Monumental Propaganda to which he contributed his own *Model for a Monument to the Third International*, completed and exhibited in 1920. Tatlin subsequently dedicated himself to designing useful objects for the new socialist society, including household items, clothing, theatrical sets and the *Letatlin* or Flying Machine which was intended to be an air bicycle, liberating Soviet man from the confines of gravity.

98 THE MONUMENT FOR THE THIRD
INTERNATIONAL 1920
Illustrated pamphlet, 21.8 x 27.9 cm
Private Collection

Vladimir Tatlin, *c*.1913

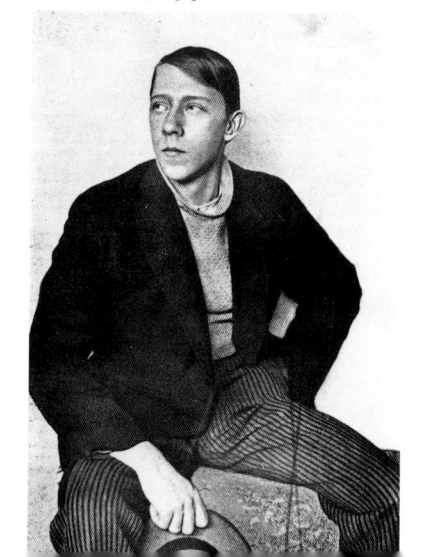

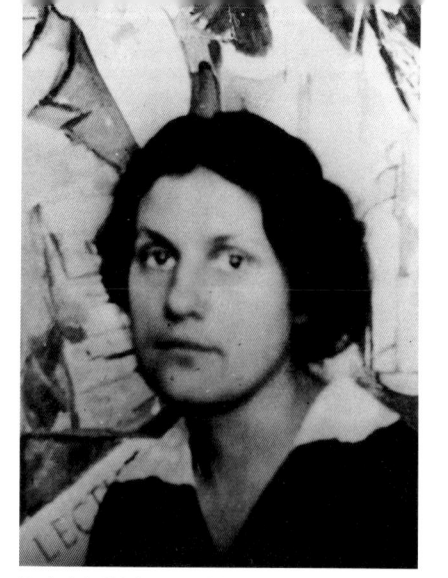

Nadezhda Udaltsova with her painting
The Restaurant, 1915

NADEZHDA UDALTSOVA 1885-1961

In 1911-12 Udaltsova visited Paris with Popova, and in 1912-13 she lived in Paris, absorbing the lessons of Cubism while studying at l'Académie la Palette with Le Fauconnier and Metzinger. She subsequently made paintings which explore the ideas of Cubism and Futurism. She came under the influence of Malevich, joining his Supremus group and producing abstract paintings of highly textured, overlapping geometric planes (1916-17). Active in IZO, Udaltsova designed decorations for the revolutionary festivals and taught at the State Free Art Studios and the VKhUTEMAS. She was a member of INKhUK, but left after the triumph of Constructivism in 1921 and returned to painting in a figurative style.

99* STILL LIFE 1916
[colour plate 30] oil on canvas, 35.5 x 44.6 cm
State Art Museum, Nizhnii Novogorod

ALEKSANDR VESNIN 1883-1959

While training as an architect, Vesnin studied in Tatlin's studio (1912-13), where he met Popova with whom he subsequently shared a studio. In the late 1910s Vesnin produced abstract paintings of densely organised overlapping planes which strongly resemble Popova's work. The two artists collaborated on the design of a revolutionary festival (1921) and taught together at the State Free Art Studios (1918-20). They were both members of INKhUK and embraced Constructivist ideas during 1921. Vesnin designed for the theatre (1920-23) and from 1922 onwards was one of the founders and principal practitioners of architectural Constructivism, working with his brothers Leonid and Viktor on projects such as the workers' clubs and buildings related to the construction of the Dneiper Dam. He also taught at the VKhUTEMAS (1920-30).

100*STUDY OF PLANES 1917
[colour plate 36] oil on canvas board, 76 x 53.5 cm
Regional Art Museum, Samara

ARTIST UNKNOWN

101 NUDE FIGURE 1918-20
oil and painted metal on wood, 52 x 22 cm
Regional Art Museum, Samara
The allusions to the hammer and sickle motif (on the chest and stomach) and the use of the colour red, suggest that this carved relief was created either as a decoration for one of the revolutionary festivals (May Day or theanniversary of the Bolshevik Revolution) or as part of Lenin's Plan of Monumental Propaganda.

Aleksandr Vesnin (photographed by Rodchenko), *c.*1924

GLOSSARY

AKHRR ASSOCIATION OF ARTISTS OF REVOLUTIONARY RUSSIA

AKhRR was set up in 1922, with a strong commitment to depict 'the events of the Revolution' and the Civil War, together with their heroes, and to celebrate contemporary achievements in industry and agriculture. AKhRR aggressively promoted what it called 'heroic realism' and attacked all formal experimentation. Supported by the Party, the group remained active and increasingly powerful until 1932 when it was abolished prior to the institution of a centrally controlled Union of Artists devoted to the theory and practice of Socialist Realism.

CONSTRUCTIVISM

Constructed sculpture, built up from separate elements of material rather than being moulded or carved, was developed by Picasso in 1912 and, in Russia, by Vladimir Tatlin in 1914. The term 'Constructivism' was initially used in March 1921 by the First Working Group of Constructivists in Moscow, which included Aleksandr Rodchenko, Aleksei Gan and Varvara Stepanova. Their aim was to participate in the construction of a post-revolutionary, socialist Russia, and they therefore rejected the autonomous art object in favour of adapting the elementary language of abstract art to designing everyday items for industrial production. In Western Europe, the International Faction of Constructivists set up in 1922 by Theo van Doesburg, Hans Richter and El Lissitzky disseminated a commitment to a clear and precise art that was collective rather than individualistic in its impulse. The international tendency of geometric abstract art, which has persisted ever since, is sometimes known as Constructivism.

Malevich (holding Suprematist plate) with members of UNOVIS, including Lissitzky, leaving Vitebsk railway station for their exhibition in Moscow, 1920

CUBO-FUTURISM

This is the term that was applied by Russian artists and critics to paintings which combined, often to very different degrees and in very different ways, various features derived from the Western movements of Cubism and Futurism. In general, it represented a creative synthesis: from Cubism it took the new ideas of pictorial space, the fragmentation of the object, and the emphasis on geometric form; from Futurism an iconoclastic ethos, an interest in urban and industrial subject-matter and a stress on the dynamism of modern experience of time and space.

INKHUK THE INSTITUTE OF ARTISTIC CULTURE

The Institute of Artistic Culture was set up in Moscow in 1920, mainly on the initiative of Wassily Kandinsky, who wrote its programme. Dedicated to investigating the language of art, the Institute rapidly moved away from the spiritual and psychological orientation of its founder to a more materialistic ethos. In Spring 1921 the Institute's debate about the distinction between the concepts of 'composition' and 'construction' in painting led to the emergence of the First Working Group of Constructivists. From 1922 until its demise in approximately 1924, the Institute was an important centre for Constructivist discussion.

IZO THE DEPARTMENT OF FINE ARTS

IZO was set up within the Commissariat for Enlightenment (Narkompros) in early 1918 in Petrograd. David Shterenberg was the head of IZO until 1921, while Vladimir Tatlin ran the Moscow section until late 1919. Between 1918 and 1921 (when IZO was reorganised), many avant-garde artists worked in its different sections for varying lengths of time.

THE KNAVE OF DIAMONDS

The group, sometimes known as The Jack of Diamonds, was primarily organised by Aristarkh Lentulov and Mikhail Larionov in late 1910. According to Ilya Mashkov, the group took its name from the diamond-shape design on the clothing of civil prisoners. This was intended to emphasise the fact that the artists also considered themselves to be social outcasts. The Knave of Diamonds held its first exhibition in December 1910, remaining active until November 1917 when it held its final show to which none of the original members contributed. In 1911 Larionov split away from the group because he found the members 'too Cézannist' and indeed the paintings of the group are known for their 'Cézannist' qualities.

MAKOVETS

Set up in 1921, Makovets emphasised the spiritual quality of art, and the importance of the art of the past in the creation of the art of the future. It organised four exhibitions (1923-6) and published three issues of a journal *Makovets* in 1922-3. Its members included artists who had formerly belonged to the Knave of Diamonds such as Aleksandr Shevchenko and others like Vera Pestel who had become disillusioned with abstraction.

NEOPRIMITIVISM

Neoprimitivism emerged during 1909 when Russian artists like Natalya Goncharova, Mikhail Larionov and David Burliuk started to assimilate and rework the lessons of French Post-Impressionism and Fauvist painting. The style developed a distinctly Russian character between 1910 and 1911 when artists sought inspiration in 'primitive' indigenous traditions: the eighteenth-century popular print, known as the *lubok*, icon painting of the fourteenth and fifteenth centuries, folk art (embroideries, painted trays, toys, etc), children's art, and the work of signpainters. The Neoprimitivists produced images of Russian life in all its manifestations that were characterised by bold colours and a consistent disregard for one-point perspective, spatial coherence and anatomical proportion.

NON-OBJECTIVE

Kazimir Malevich used the term *bespredmetnoe* which literally means 'without objects' or 'objectless' to denote the complete absence of legible subject-matter in his paintings and to convey the idea that the work of art was created from purely pictorial elements rather than from objects derived from the world of natural appearances. Other Russian artists followed his lead, preferring this term to the more ambiguous 'abstract', with its connotations of simplifying or in some other way transforming an observed or imagined image.

NOZH THE NEW SOCIETY OF PAINTERS

Formally organised in 1922, the group had six members including Samuil Adlivankin. The group only held one exhibition in Moscow in 1922. The catalogue contained the declaration 'Our Path' which called for 'Painting that is objective and realistic'. In 1924 NOZH was officially dissolved.

Kandinsky with members of Narkompros including Falk (extreme left), Moscow *c.*1920

OST THE SOCIETY OF EASEL PAINTERS

Formally established in 1925, OST was active until 1931. The majority of its members were graduates from the VKhUTEMAS, many having studied with David Shterenberg who was a founder member. The group was committed to 'absolute technical mastery in the field of easel painting, drawing and sculpture' while also espousing 'Revolutionary contemporaneity and clarity of subject-matter'.

RAYISM

Described as a synthesis of Cubism, Futurism and Orphism, Rayism sought to depict 'the spatial forms arising from the intersection of the reflected rays of various objects'. It was developed during 1912 by Mikhail Larionov who exhibited his first works in this style towards the end of the year and presented it as a fully developed method at the Target Exhibition in the spring of 1913. In the essentially linear configurations of 'Realistic Rayism', the objects from which the rays emanate are still fairly legible, but in the later 'Pneumo-Rayism', the pictorial elements are far more independent of external reality, often becoming completely abstract.

SUPREMATISM

Suprematism was developed by Kazimir Malevich in Russia during 1915 and launched in December that year when he exhibited thirty-nine Suprematist paintings including *The Black Rectangle* (better known as *The Black Square*) at the 0.10 (Zero-Ten) Exhibition in Petrograd. Suprematism, which he defined as the 'painting of pure form' and 'the supremacy of pure feeling', comprised dynamic configurations of geometric planes flatly painted against white grounds. Subsequently, Malevich developed paintings of single forms which fade into the white grounds and *c*. 1918 started to paint his series of white on white paintings which create an even stronger sensation of immateriality and infinite space. In 1919 at Vitebsk he established a group called UNOVIS (Affirmers of the New Art) which was dedicated to using the principles of Suprematism to transform the environment.

Students in the metalworking faculty of the VKhUTEMAS, early 1920s

THE UNION OF YOUTH

Founded in St Petersburg in 1909, the Union of Youth held several exhibitions between May 1910 and January 1914 when it ceased activity. Numerous artists including Kazimir Malevich, Vladimir Tatlin, Olga Rozanova, Pavel Filonov, Marc Chagall, Mikhail Matyushin, and Alexandra Exter contributed to the group's shows. Led by the artist and theoretician Vladimir Markov, who wrote extensively on *faktura* (texture) and primitive art, the group also stimulated considerable discussion about the new aesthetic possibilities at its public debates and in its journal, *The Union of Youth*, three issues of which appeared between 1912 and 1913.

VKHUTEMAS

VKhUTEMAS grew out of the State Free Art Studios. These had been set up in Moscow in 1918 on the basis of the existing art schools. Tuition was free to all, and students could choose their own teachers from the staff, which included Wassily Kandinsky, Kazimir Malevich and Vladimir Tatlin. In December 1920 the Studios were reorganised into the VKhUTEMAS, the Higher Artistic and Technical Workshops, which had a more disciplined and industrial orientation. Lyubov Popova, Aleksandr Vesnin, Aleksandr Rodchenko, Varvara Stepanova, and later Tatlin and El Lissitzky were all involved in developing teaching programmes at the school in accordance with the tenets of Constructivism. Reorganised and renamed the VKhUTEIN (the Higher Artistic and Technical Institute) in 1927, the school was eventually closed in 1930.

GENERAL

Alan Bird, *A History of Russian Painting*, Phaidon, Oxford, 1987.

John E. Bowlt, ed., and trans., *Russian Art of the Avant-Garde: Theory and Criticism*, Thames and Hudson, London, 1988.

Jeremy Howard, *The Union of Youth: An Artists' Society of the Russian Avant-Garde*, Manchester University Press, 1992.

Angelica Rudenstine, ed., *Russian Avant-Garde Art: The George Costakis Collection*, Thames and Hudson, London, 1981.

Dmitri V. Sarabianov, *Russian Art: From Neoclassicisim to the Avant-Garde: Painting, Sculpture, Architecture*, Thames and Hudson, London, 1990.

The Great Utopia: The Russian and Soviet Avant-Garde 1915-1932, Solomon R. Guggenheim Museum, New York, 1992.

SUPREMATISM

Larissa Zhadova, *Kazimir Malevich: Suprematism and Revolution in Russian Art 1910-1930*, Thames and Hudson, London, 1982.

CONSTRUCTIVISM

Art into Life, Henry Art Gallery, Seattle, and Rizzoli, New York, 1990.

Christina Lodder, *Russian Constructivism*, Yale University Press, London and Newhaven, 1983.

CHAGALL

Susan Compton, *Chagall,* Royal Academy of Arts, London, 1985.

Aleksandr Kamensky, *Chagall: The Russian Years 1907-1922*, Thames and Hudson, London, 1989.

EXTER

Alexandra Exter e il Teatro da Camera, Electa, Milan, 1991.

Andrei B. Nakov, *Alexandra Exter*, Galerie Jean Chauvelin, Paris, 1972.

FILONOV

Trans., ed., Nicoletta Misler and John E. Bowlt, *Pavel Filonov: A Hero And His Fate*, Silvergirl Inc., Austin, Texas, 1984.

GONCHAROVA

Mary Chamot, *Goncharova: Stage Designs and Paintings*, Oresko Books Limited, London, 1979.

LARIONOV

Waldemar George, *Larionov*, Bibliothèque des Arts, Paris, 1966.

KANDINSKY

Kenneth Lindsay and Peter Vergo, eds., *Kandinsky: Complete Writings on Art*, Faber and Faber, London, 1982.

Rose-Carol Washton Long, *Kandinsky: The Development of an Abstract Style*, Clarendon Press, Oxford, 1980.

LISSITZKY

Sophie Lissitzky-Küppers, *El Lissitzky: Life, Letters, Texts*, Thames and Hudson, London, 1968.

El Lissitzky 1890-1941: Architect, Painter, Photographer, Typographer, Thames and Hudson, London, 1990.

MALEVICH

Trans., Xenia Glowacki-Prus and Arnold McMillin, ed., Troels Andersen, *K.S. Malevich: Essays on Art 1915-1933*, 2 vols, Rapp and Whiting, London, 1971.

Trans., Xenia Glowacki-Prus and Edmund T. Little, ed., Troels Andersen, *K.S. Malevich: The World as Non-Objectivity: Unpublished Writings 1922-5*, Borgens Forlag, Copenhagen, 1976.

Trans., Xenia Glowacki-Prus, ed., Troels Andersen, *K. S. Malevich: The Artist, Infinity, Suprematism: Unpublished Writings 1913-33*, Borgens Forlag, Copenhagen, 1978.

Charlotte Douglas, *Swans of Other Worlds: Kazimir Malevich and the Origins of Abstraction in Russia*, UMI Research Press, Ann Arbor, 1980.

Kazimir Malevich 1878-1935, Armand Hammer Museum of Art and Cultural Center, Los Angeles, 1990.

POPOVA

Magdalena Dabrowski, *Liubov Popova*, Museum of Modern Art, New York, 1991.

RODCHENKO

Selim O. Khan-Magomedov, *Rodchenko: The Complete Work*, Thames and Hudson, London, 1986.

ROZANOVA

Olga Rozanova 1886-1918, Helsingin Kaupungin Taideomuseo, Helsinki, 1992.

TATLIN

John Milner, *Vladimir Tatlin and the Russian Avant-Garde*, Yale University Press, London and New Haven, 1983.

Larissa Zhadova, ed., *Vladimir Tatlin*, Thames and Hudson, London, 1989.